ROGER MCGOUGH

The Ring of Words

An anthology of poetry for children

illustrated by SATOSHI KITAMURA

faber and faber

First published in 1998
by Faber and Faber Limited
3 Queen Square London WC1N 3AU

This paperback edition first published in 1999

Photoset by Wilmaset Ltd, Wirral
Printed and bound in Great Britain by
Butler & Tanner Ltd, Frome and London

A CIP record for this book
is available from the British Library

ISBN 0–571–19736–1

10 9 8 7 6 5 4 3 2 1

I am the song. I am very fond of bananas. Whee!

N ouns like noses, nettles and night

T ricks that'll tickle and tygers bright

R ed boots and riddles, rhinos and raths

O zymandias, owls and overgrown paths

D azzlers, dunces, donkeys and dancers

U ntamed underpants, unlikely answers

C ats and cabbages, cold feet and coves

T ailspins and treetops and Yuk! slithy toves

I am a Poet. I can eat saucepans. Whee!

O odle ardle wardle, that's enough from me

N ow off you go and read the poems.

Contents

The Ring of Words

My Name Is ...

Chalks of Many Colours

A Stranger Called this Morning

Be Like the Bird

Thoughts like an Ocean

Kicking Up the Winter

Conservation Piece

Escape at Bedtime

Benediction

The Ring of Words

Words

Bright is the ring of words
    When the right man rings them,
Fair the fall of songs
    When the singer sings them.
Still they are carolled and said –
    On wings they are carried –
After the singer is dead
    And the maker buried.

Robert Louis Stevenson

I am the Song

I am the song that sings the bird.
I am the leaf that grows the land.
I am the tide that moves the moon.
I am the stream that halts the sand.
I am the cloud that drives the storm.
I am the earth that lights the sun.
I am the fire that strikes the stone.
I am the clay that shapes the hand.
I am the word that speaks the man.

Charles Causley

An Ordinary Day

I took my mind a walk
Or my mind took me a walk –
Whichever was the truth of it.

The light glittered on the water
Or the water glittered in the light.
Cormorants stood on a tidal rock

With their wings spread out,
Stopping no traffic. Various ducks
Shilly-shallied here and there

On the shilly-shallying water.
An occasional gull yelped. Small flowers
Were doing their level best

To bring to their kerb bees like
Aerial charabancs. Long weeds in the clear
Water did Eastern dances, unregarded

By shoals of darning needles. A cow
Started a moo but thought
Better of it ... And my feet took me home

And my mind observed to me,
Or I to it, how ordinary
Extraordinary things are or

How extraordinary ordinary
Things are, like the nature of the mind
And the process of observing.

Norman MacCaig

The Word Party

Loving words clutch crimson roses,
Rude words sniff and pick their noses,
Sly words come dressed up as foxes,
Short words stand on cardboard boxes,
Common words tell jokes and gabble,
Complicated words play Scrabble,
Swear words stamp around and shout,
Hard words stare each other out,
Foreign words look lost and shrug,
Careless words trip on the rug,
Long words slough with stooping shoulders,
Code words carry secret folders,
Silly words flick rubber bands,
Hyphenated words hold hands,
Strong words show off, bending metal,
Sweet words call each other 'petal',
Small words yawn and suck their thumbs
Till at last the morning comes.
Kind words give out farewell posies ...

Snap! The dictionary closes.

Richard Edwards

The All-Purpose Children's Poem

The first verse contains a princess
    Two witches (one evil, one good)
There is a castle in it somewhere
    And a dark and tangled wood.

The second has ghosts and vampires
    Monsters with foul-smelling breath
It sends shivers down the book spine
    And scares everybody to death.

The third is one of my favourites
    With rabbits in skirts and trousers
Who talk to each other like we do
    And live in neat little houses.

The fourth verse is bang up to date
    And in it anything goes.
Set in the city, it doesn't rhyme
    (Although, in a way it does).

The fifth is set in the future
    (And as you can see, it's the last)
When the Word was made Computer
    And books are a thing of the past.

Roger McGough

First Echo

I recall the high trees rocking in the wind,
across the road where the soldiers drilled.
They learned their trades there, and went to war.
Beyond was unknown country, fields and distance
where the sun went out.
            One day my shout
among the tall trees found its echo there,
bouncing my name back among the elms,
calling and calling at the house back
and a second out of time the voice of *not-me*,
repeating all I said though what I said
was only *I, I, I am* ...

How does anyone write anything?
How do they begin, in what gesture,
in what moment of prayer, the pen
to the paper? What would anybody say?

    Ken Smith

Echo

'Who called?' I said, and the words
   Through the whispering glades,
Hither, thither, baffled the birds –
   'Who called? Who called?'

The leafy boughs on high
   Hissed in the sun;
The dark air carried my cry
   Faintingly on:

Eyes in the green, in the shade,
   In the motionless brake,
Voices that said what I said,
   For mockery's sake:

'Who cares?' I bawled through my tears:
   The wind fell low:
In the silence, 'Who cares? who cares?'
   Wailed to and fro.

Walter de la Mare

Question

Who else could ever
Fit into this head

Look through these holes,
And see this particular view?
Robert Shure

Hendecasyllables

It is the very bewitching hour of eight
Which is the moment when my new day begins,
I love to hear the pretty clock striking eight
I love to get up out of my bed quickly.
Why is this? Because morning air is so cold?
Or because of new strength that seems to come then?
Both. And also because waking up ends dreams.

Stevie Smith

Myrtle

There once was a girl named Myrtle
Who, strangely enough, *was* a Turtle:
She was mad as a Hare,
She could growl like a Bear, –
O *No*body understood Myrtle!

She would sit with a Book on her Knees, –
My Poetry-Book, if you please, –
She'd Rant and She'd Roar:
'This stuff is a Bore!
Why I could do better
With only ONE Letter, –
These Poets, they write like *I* Sneeze!'

Theodore Roethke

Little Girl, Be Careful What You Say

Little girl, be careful what you say
when you make talk with words, words –
for words are made of syllables
and syllables, child, are made of air –
and air is so thin – air is the breath of God –
air is finer than fire or mist,
finer than water or moonlight,
finer than spider-webs in the moon,
finer than water-flowers in the morning:
   and words are strong, too,
   stronger than rocks or steel
stronger than potatoes, corn, fish, cattle,
and soft, too, soft as little pigeon eggs,
soft as the music of hummingbird wings.
   So, little girl, when you speak greetings,
when you tell jokes, make wishes or prayers,
   be careful, be careless, be careful,
   be what you wish to be.

Carl Sandburg

Unfolding Bud

One is amazed
By a water-lily bud
Unfolding
With each passing day,
Taking on a richer color
And new dimensions.

One is not amazed,
At a first glance,
By a poem,
Which is as tight-closed
As a tiny bud.

Yet one is surprised
To see the poem
Gradually unfolding,
Revealing its rich inner self,
As one reads it
Again
And over again.

Naoshi Koriyama

'And What,' Said the Emperor

'And what,' said the Emperor, 'does this poem describe?'
'It describes,' said the Poet, 'the cave of the Never-Never,
Would you like to see what's inside?' He offered his arm.
They stepped into the poem and disappeared forever.

George Barker

Strange Story

I saw a pigeon making bread
I saw a girl composed of thread
I saw a towel one mile square
I saw a meadow in the air
I saw a rocket walk a mile
I saw a pony make a file
I saw a blacksmith in a box
I saw an orange kill an ox
I saw a butcher made of steel
I saw a penknife dance a reel
I saw a sailor twelve feet high
I saw a ladder in a pie
I saw an apple fly away
I saw a sparrow making hay
I saw a farmer like a dog
I saw a puppy mixing grog
I saw three men who saw these too
And will confirm what I tell you.

Anonymous

(The secret of this poem is to stop in the *middle* of each line.)

Have You Ever Seen

Have you ever seen a sheet on a river bed?
Or a single hair from a hammer's head?
Has the foot of a mountain any toes?
And is there a pair of garden hose?

Does the needle ever wink its eye?
Why doesn't the wing of a building fly?
Can you tickle the ribs of a parasol?
Or open the trunk of a tree at all?

Are the teeth of a rake ever going to bite?
Have the hands of a clock any left or right?
Can the garden plot be deep and dark?
And what is the sound of the birch's bark?

Anonymous

Where?

where do you hide a leaf?
in, if possib*le, a f*orest.

where do you hide a wind?
among stra*w in d*ust.

where do you hide a horse?
within clo*th or se*a.

where do you hide the sun?
behind cloud*s, un*der horizons.

where do you hide water?
belo*w a ter*rible flood.

where do you hide a storm?
inside a gho*st or m*agician.

where do you hide a word?

Dave Calder

Poemology

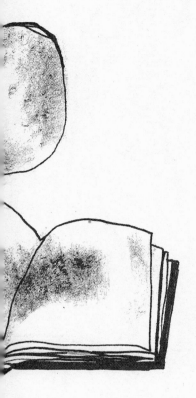

an apple a day
is 365 apples

a poem a day
is 365 poems
most years

any doctor will tell you
it is easier to eat an apple
than to make a poem

it is also easier
to eat a poem
than to make an apple
but only
just.

   but here
is what you do
to keep the doctor
out of it:

          publish a poem
on your appletree

have an apple
in your next book

Anselm Hollo

The Uncertainty of the Poet

I am a poet.
I am very fond of bananas.

I am bananas.
I am very fond of a poet.

I am a poet of bananas.
I am very fond.

A fond poet of 'I am, I am' –
Very bananas.

Fond of 'Am I bananas?
Am I?' – a very poet.

Bananas of a poet!
Am I fond? Am I very?

Poet bananas! I am.
I am fond of a 'very'.

I am of very fond bananas.
Am I a poet?

Wendy Cope

Wish in Spring

Today I wish that I were a tree,
And not myself,
Confronting spring with a neat little row of poems
Like cups and saucers on a shelf.

For then I should have poems innumerable,
One kissing the other;
Authentic, perfect in shape and lovely variety,
And all of the same tireless green colour.

No one would think it unnatural
Or question my right;
All day I would wave them above the heads of the people,
And sing them to myself all night.

But as I am only a woman
And not a tree,
With piteous human care I have made this poem,
And set it now on the shelf with the rest to be.

Sylvia Townsend Warner

Poem for a dead poet

He was a poet he was.
A proper poet.
He said things
that made you think
and said them nicely.
He saw things
that you or I
could never see
and saw them clearly.
He had a way
with language.
Images flocked around
him like birds,
St Francis, he was,
of the words. Words?
Why he could almost make 'em talk.

Roger McGough

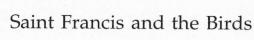

Saint Francis and the Birds

When Francis preached love to the birds
They listened, fluttered, throttled up
Into the blue like a flock of words

Released for fun from his holy lips.
Then wheeled back, whirred about his head,
Pirouetted on brothers' capes,

Danced on the wing, for sheer joy played
And sang, like images took flight.
Which was the best poem Francis made,

His argument true, his tone light.

Seamus Heaney

The New Poem

It will not resemble the sea.
It will not have dirt on its thick hands.
It will not be part of the weather.
It will not reveal its name.

It will not have dreams you can count on.
It will not be photogenic.

It will not attend our sorrow.
It will not console our children.
It will not be able to help us.

Charles Wright

Deeds not Words

A man of words and not of deeds
Is like a garden full of weeds;

And when the weeds begin to grow,
It's like a garden full of snow;

And when the snow begins to fall,
It is like birds upon a wall;

And when the birds begin to fly,
It's like a shipwreck in the sky;

And when the sky begins to roar,
It's like a lion at the door;

And when the door begins to crack,
It's like a stick across your back;

And when your back begins to smart,
It's like a penknife in your heart;

And when your heart begins to bleed,
Oh then you're dead and dead indeed!

Anonymous

Playing a Dazzler

You bash drums playing a dazzler;
I worry a trumpet swaying with it.

You dance, you make a girl's skirt swirl;
I dance, I dance by myself.

You bowl, I lash air and my wicket;
I bowl, you wallop boundary balls.

Your goal-kick beat me between my knees;
my goal-kick flies into a pram-and-baby.

You eat off your whole-pound chocolate cake;
I swell up halfway to get my mate's help.

My bike hurls me into the hedge;
your bike swerves half-circle from trouble.

I jump the wall and get dumped;
you leap over the wall and laugh, satisfied.

I touch the country bridge and walk;
you talk and talk.

You write poems with line-end rhymes;
I write poems with rhymes nowhere or anywhere.

Your computer game screens monsters and gunners;
my game brings on swimmers and courting red birds.

James Berry

My Name Is ...

My name is Sluggery-wuggery
My name is Worms-for-tea
My name is Swallow-the-table-leg
My name is Drink-the-Sea.

My name is I-eat-saucepans
My name is I-like-snails
My name is Grand-piano-George
My name is I-ride-whales.

My name is Jump-the-chimney
My name is Bite-my-knee
My name is Jiggery-pokery
And Riddle-me-ree, and ME.

Pauline Clarke

One

Only one of me
and nobody can get a second one
from a photocopy machine.

Nobody has the fingerprints I have.
Nobody can cry my tears, or laugh my laugh
or have my expectancy when I wait.

But anybody can mimic my dance with my dog.
Anybody can howl how I sing out of tune.
And mirrors can show me multiplied
many times, say , dressed up in red
or dressed up in grey.

Nobody can get into my clothes for me
or feel my fall for me, or do my running.
Nobody hears my music for me, either.

I am just this one.
Nobody else makes the words
I shape with sound, when I talk.

But anybody can act how I stutter in a rage.
Anybody can copy echoes I make.
And mirrors can show me multiplied
many times, say, dressed up in green
or dressed up in blue.

James Berry

Two of Everything

My friend Shola said to me that she said to her mum:
'It's not fair, Carla (that's me) has two of everything:

Carla has two bedrooms,
two sets of toys, two telephones,

two wardrobes, two door mats,
two mummies, two cats,

two water purifiers, two kitchens,
two environmentally friendly squeezies.'

My friend Shola said to me that she said to her mum:
'Why can't you and Dad get divorced?'

But the thing Shola doesn't even realize yet,
is that there are two of me.

Jackie Kay

My Little Eye

The cord of my new dressing-gown
he helps me tie

Then on to my father's shoulder
held high

The world at night with my little eye
I spy

The moon close enough to touch
I try

Unheard of silver elephants have learned
to fly

Giants fence with searchlights
in the sky

Too soon into the magic shelter
he and I

Air raids are so much fun
I wonder why

In the bunk below, a big boy
starts to cry.

Roger McGough

The Visitors

Little brother you'll never guess what.
The aliens have just landed.
No they don't have pointed ears
but they are armed and handed.

No they don't have suckers.
No not red blue yellow or green.
But all in black and silver
and one keeps a talking machine

in a special secret pocket.
You can see the blue light out there
well it comes from their rocket.
You can hear their voices downstairs

they're talking to Da that's right.
They want to know where he was
on the planet Earth last night
between seven and ten because

how should I know?
Ma says they'll go away soon
but if you ask me I don't think so.
I think they'll take Da to the moon.

No they are not friendly.
No you can't go downstairs.
I will protect you don't worry.
Move over.

Brian McCabe

The Shoes

These are the shoes
Dad walked about in
When we did jobs
In the garden,
When his shed
Was full of shavings,
When he tried
To put the fence up,
When my old bike
Needed mending,
When the car
Could not get started,
When he got up late
On Sunday.
These are the shoes
Dad walked about in
And I've kept them
In my room.

These are not the shoes
That Dad walked out in
When we didn't know
Where he was going,
When I tried to lift
His suitcase,
When he said goodbye
And kissed me,
When he left his door-key
On the table,
When he promised Mum
He'd send a postcard,

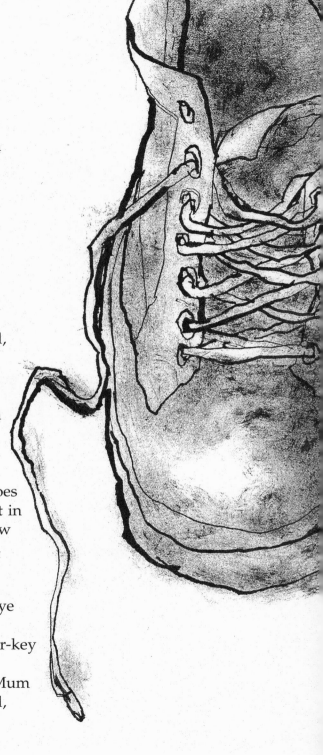

When I couldn't hear
His special footsteps.
These are not the shoes
That Dad walked out in
But he'll need them
When he comes back home.

John Mole

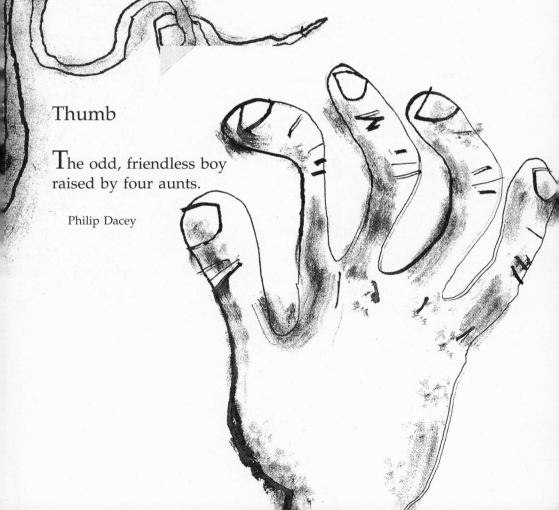

Thumb

The odd, friendless boy
raised by four aunts.

Philip Dacey

Three Brothers

I had Three Brothers,
Harold and Robert and James,
All of them tall and handsome,
All of them good at games.
And I was allowed to field for them,
To bowl to them, to score:
I was allowed to slave for them
For ever and evermore.
Oh, I was allowed to fetch and carry for my Three Brothers,
Jim and Bob and Harry.

All of my brothers,
Harry and Jim and Bob,
Grew to be good and clever,
Each of them at his job.
And I was allowed to wait on them,
To be their slave complete,
I was allowed to work for them
And life for me was sweet,
For I was allowed to fetch and carry for my Three Brothers,
Jim and Bob and Harry.

Jim went out to South Africa,
Bob went out to Ceylon,
Harry went out to New Zealand
And settled in Wellington.
And the grass grew high on the cricket-pitch,
And the tennis-court went to hay,
And the place was too big and too silent
After they went away.

So I turned it into a Guest House,
After our parents died,

And I wrote to the boys every Sunday,
And once a year they replied.
All of them married eventually,
I wrote to their wives, of course,
And their wives wrote back on postcards –
Well ... it might have been very much worse.

And now I have nine nieces,
Most of them home at school.
I have them all to stay here
For the holidays, as a rule.
And I am allowed to slave for them,
To do odd jobs galore,
I am allowed to work for them
And life is sweet once more,
For I am allowed to fetch and carry for the children of
Jim and Bob and Harry.

Joyce Grenfell

A Recollection

My father's friend came once to tea.
He laughed and talked. He spoke to me.
But in another week they said
That friendly pink-faced man was dead.

'How sad . . .' they said, 'the best of men . . .'
So I said too, 'How sad'; but then
Deep in my heart, I thought, with pride,
'I know a person who has died.'

Frances Cornford

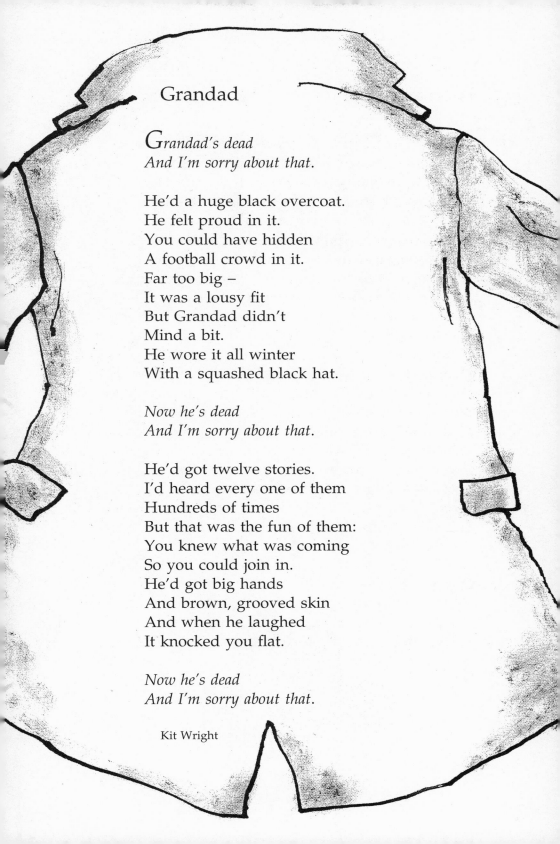

Grandad

Grandad's dead
And I'm sorry about that.

He'd a huge black overcoat.
He felt proud in it.
You could have hidden
A football crowd in it.
Far too big –
It was a lousy fit
But Grandad didn't
Mind a bit.
He wore it all winter
With a squashed black hat.

Now he's dead
And I'm sorry about that.

He'd got twelve stories.
I'd heard every one of them
Hundreds of times
But that was the fun of them:
You knew what was coming
So you could join in.
He'd got big hands
And brown, grooved skin
And when he laughed
It knocked you flat.

Now he's dead
And I'm sorry about that.

Kit Wright

Hide and Seek

Call out. Call loud: 'I'm ready! Come and find me!'
The sacks in the toolshed smell like the seaside.
They'll never find you in this salty dark,
But be careful that your feet aren't sticking out.
Wiser not to risk another shout.
The floor is cold. They'll probably be searching
The bushes near the swing. Whatever happens
You mustn't sneeze when they come prowling in.
And here they are, whispering at the door;
You've never heard them sound so hushed before.
Don't breathe. Don't move. Stay dumb. Hide in your
    blindness.
They're moving closer, someone stumbles, mutters;
Their words and laughter scuffle, and they're gone.
But don't come out just yet; they'll try the lane
And then the greenhouse and back here again.
They must be thinking that you're very clever,
Getting more puzzled as they search all over.
It seems a long time since they went away.
Your legs are stiff, the cold bites through your coat;
The dark damp smell of sand moves in your throat.
It's time to let them know that you're the winner.
Push off the sacks. Uncurl and stretch. That's better!
Out of the shed and call to them: 'I've won!
Here I am! Come and own up I've caught you!'
The darkening garden watches. Nothing stirs.
The bushes hold their breath; the sun is gone.
Yes, here you are. But where are they who sought you?

Vernon Scannell

A Boy

Half a mile from the sea,
in a house with a dozen bedrooms
he grew up. Who was he?
Oh, nobody much. A boy
with the usual likes
and more than a few dislikes.
Did he swim much? Nah,
that sea was the Atlantic
and out there is *Ice*land.
He kept his play inland
on an L-shaped football pitch
between the garage and the gate.
What did he eat?
Stuff his grandfather made,
home-made sausages,
potted pig's head.
He got the library keys
and carried eight books at a time
home, and he read.
He read so much
He stayed in the book's world.
Wind rattled the window
of his third-storey room,
but his bed was warm.
And he stayed in his bed
half the day if he could,
reading by candlelight
when the storms struck
and the electricity died.
How do I know all this?
You'd guess how if you tried.

Matthew Sweeney

It Was Long Ago

I'll tell you, shall I, something I remember?
Something that still means a great deal to me.
It was long ago.

A dusty road in summer I remember,
A mountain, and an old house, and a tree
That stood, you know,

Behind the house. An old woman I remember
In a red shawl with a grey cat on her knee
Humming under a tree.

She seemed the oldest thing I can remember,
But then perhaps I was not more than three.
It was long ago.

I dragged on the dusty road, and I remember
How the old woman looked over the fence at me
And seemed to know

How it felt to be three, and called out, I remember
'Do you like bilberries and cream for tea?'
I went under the tree

And while she hummed, and the cat purred, I remember
How she filled a saucer with berries and cream for me
So long ago,

Such berries and such cream as I remember
I never had seen before, and never see
Today, you know.

And that is almost all I can remember,
The house, the mountain, the grey cat on her knee,
Her red shawl, and the tree,

And the taste of the berries, the feel of the sun I remember,
And the smell of everything that used to be
So long ago,

Till the heat on the road outside again I remember,
And how the long dusty road seemed to have for me
No end, you know.

That is the farthest thing I can remember.
It won't mean much to you. It does to me.
Then I grew up, you see.

    Eleanor Farjeon

You Can't Be That

I told them:
When I grow up
I'm not going to be a scientist
Or someone who reads the news on TV.
No, a million birds will fly through me.
I'M GOING TO BE A TREE!

They said,
You can't be that. No, you can't be that.

I told them:
When I grow up
I'm not going to be an airline pilot,
A dancer, a lawyer or an MC.
No, huge whales will swim in me.
I'M GOING TO BE AN OCEAN!

They said,
You can't be that. No, you can't be that.

I told them:
I'm not going to be a DJ,
A computer programmer, a musician or beautician.
No, streams will flow through me, I'll be the home of eagles;
I'll be full of nooks, crannies, valleys and fountains.
I'M GOING TO BE A RANGE OF MOUNTAINS!

They said,
You can't be that. No, you can't be that.

I asked them:
Just what do you think I am?
Just a child, they said,
And children always become
At least one of the things
We want them to be.

They do not understand me.
I'll be a stable if I want, smelling of fresh hay,
I'll be a lost glade in which unicorns still play.
They do not realize I can fulfil any ambition.
They do not realize among them
Walks a magician.

Brian Patten

A Small Girl Swinging

When first they pushed me
  I was very scared.
My tummy jiggled. I was
  Unprepared.

The second time was higher
  And my ears
Were cold with whisperings
  Of tiny fears.

The third time up was HIGH,
  My teeth on edge.
My heart leapt off the bedroom
  Window ledge.

The fourth time, Oh, the fourth time
  It was mad.
My shirt flew off the world
  And I was glad.

No one's pushing now,
  My ears are ringing.
Who'll see across the park
  A small girl swinging?

Who'll hear across the park
  Her mother calling,
And everywhere her shadows
  Rising, falling?

George Szirtes

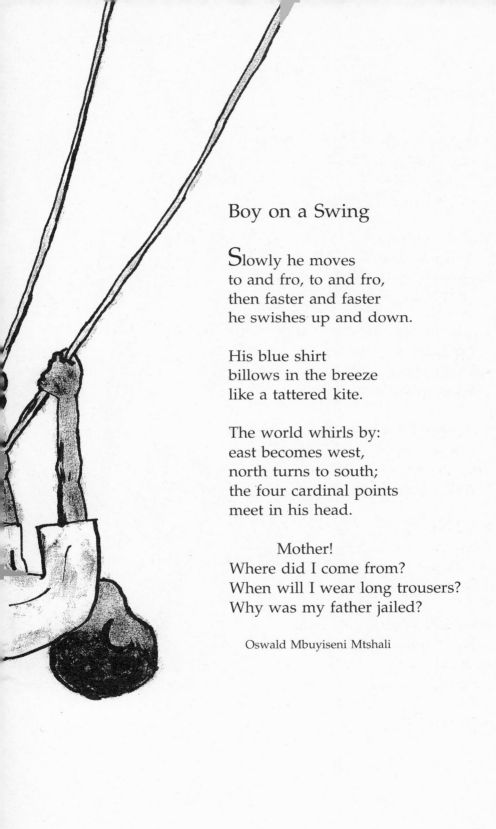

Boy on a Swing

Slowly he moves
to and fro, to and fro,
then faster and faster
he swishes up and down.

His blue shirt
billows in the breeze
like a tattered kite.

The world whirls by:
east becomes west,
north turns to south;
the four cardinal points
meet in his head.

    Mother!
Where did I come from?
When will I wear long trousers?
Why was my father jailed?

Oswald Mbuyiseni Mtshali

Whee!

I held my head in both hands
and flung it through the air.
Borne by the wind it soared away,
streaming out my hair.

The world from high perspectives looked
duller than ditchwater.
I rose above its dreariness,
Halley's Comet's daughter.

Higher than the flightpaths of dreams,
my cranium sped on.
Whilst, down below, the people said
She's crazy. Head's gone.

It's easy! Just shrug your shoulders,
turn your mind to the sky.
Then throw you head like a beachball.
Whee! Goodbye ... Goodbye ...

Carol Ann Duffy

I Am Falling off a Mountain

I am falling off a mountain,
I am plummeting through space,
you may see this does not please me
by the frown upon my face.

As the ground keeps getting nearer,
it's a simple task to tell
that I've got a slight dilemma, –
that my day's not going well.

My velocity's increasing,
I am dropping like a stone,
I could do with some assistance,
is there someone I can phone?

Though I'm unafraid of falling,
I am prompted to relate
that the landing has me worried,
and I don't have long to wait.

I am running out of options,
there's just one thing left to try –
in the next eleven seconds,
I have got to learn to fly!

   Jack Prelutsky

The Tailspin

Going into a tailspin
in those days meant curtains.
No matter how hard you pulled back on the stick
the nose of the plane wouldn't come up.

Spinning round, headed for a target of earth,
the whine of death in the wing struts,
instinct made you try to pull out of it that way, by force,
and for years aviators spiraled down and crashed.

Who could have dreamed that the solution
to this dreaded aeronautical problem
was so simple?
Every student flier learns this nowadays:
You move the joystick in the direction of the spin
and like a miracle the plane stops turning
and you are in control again
to pull the nose up out of the dive.

In panic we want to push the stick away from the spin,
wrestle the plane out of it,
but the trick is, as in everything,
to go with the turning willingly,
rather than fight, give in, go with it,
and that way come out of your tailspin whole.

Edward Field

Cabbages

When I awake, I'm at the center of a cabbage.
All is deep green
                    and unmistakably
cabbage.
No matter how easy a cabbage is to peel,
leaf by leaf,
from the outside,
there is no way to get
out
once you are
in.
So
you sing all the songs you know
and hum all the songs
you don't know
and wait for a rabbit
or someone
to come along
and look at the strange cabbage
with a voice
that sings.

Karen Slotnick

The Radio Men

When I was little more than six
I thought that men must be
Alive inside the radio
To act in plays, or simply blow
Trumpets, or sing to me.

I never got a glimpse of them,
They were so very small.
But I imagined them in there,
Their voices bursting on the air
Through that thin, wooden wall.

Elizabeth Jennings

The Railway Children

When we climbed the slopes of the cutting
We were eye level with the white cups
Of the telegraph poles and the sizzling wires.

Like lovely freehand they curved for miles
East and miles west beyond us, sagging
Under their burden of swallows.

We were small and thought we knew nothing
Worth knowing. We thought words travelled the wires
In the shiny pouches of raindrops,

Each one seeded full with the light
Of the sky, the gleam of the lines, and ourselves
So infinitesimally scaled

We could stream through the eye of a needle.

Seamus Heaney

Cold Feet

They have all gone across
They are all turning to see
They are all shouting 'come on'
They are all waiting for me.

I look through the gaps in the footway
And my heart shrivels with fear,
For far below the river is flowing
So quick and so cold and so clear.

And all that there is between it
And me falling down there is this:
A few wooden planks – not very thick –
And between each, a little abyss.

The holes get right under my sandals.
I can see straight through to the rocks,
And if I don't look, I can feel it,
Just there, through my shoes and my socks.

Suppose my feet and my legs withered up
And slipped through the slats like a rug?
Suppose I suddenly went very thin
Like the baby that slid down the plug?

I know that it cannot happen
But suppose that it did, what then?
Would they be able to find me
And take me back home again?

They have all gone across
They are all waiting to see
They are all shouting 'come on' –
But they'll have to carry me.

Brian Lee

I Stepped from Plank to Plank

I stepped from plank to plank,
A slow and cautious way;
The stars about my head I felt,
About my feet the sea.

I knew not but the next
Would be my final inch.
This gave me that precarious gait
Some call experience.

Emily Dickinson

Manco the Peruvian Chief

i looked down at my stomach
the way one does
in the bath
and noticed that i was scarlet
from head to toe
good gracious
i gasped
now i am a redskin
i am hiawatha
pocahontas
sitting bull
and manco the peruvian chief
i live in a forest of tall spruce
and sleep at night
in a wigwam full of strange odours
and wood smoke
hist
i hear pale faces in the lounge
powwowing with my squaw
curse the whites
uttering fierce battle cries
i charged down stairs
and whooped into the meeting house
indian brave no likum pale face
i shouted defiantly
ho
ho
ho
mother hastily threw a rug around me
and said

excuse me ladies
i think julian has measles

for two weeks i never left my bed
and was waited on
hand
and foot

Redmond Phillips

Attention Seeking

I'm needing attention.
I know I'm needing attention
because I hear people say it.
People that know these things.
I'm needing attention,
so what I'll do is steal something.
I know I'll steal something
because that is what I do
when I'm needing attention.

Or else I'll mess up my sister's room,
throw all her clothes on to the floor,
put her gerbil under her pillow
and lay a trap above the door (terrible)
a big heavy dictionary to drop on her
when she comes through. (Swot.)
This is the kind of thing I do
when I'm needing attention.
But I'm never boring.
I always think up new things.
Attention has lots of colours
and tunes. And lots of punishments.
For attention you can get detention.
Extra homework. Extra housework.
All sorts of things. Although
yesterday I heard the woman say
that I was just needing
someone to listen. My dad went mad.
'Listen to him!' he said, 'Listen!
You've got to be joking.'
Mind you, that was right after
I stole his car keys and drove
his car straight into the wall.
I wasn't hurt, but I'm still
needing quite a lot of attention.

Jackie Kay

Why Must We Go to School?

Why must we go to school, dad?
Tell us, dear daddy, do.
Give us your thoughts on this problem, please;
No one knows better than you.

To prepare for life, my darling child,
Or so it seems to me;
And stop you all from running wild –
Now, shut up and eat your tea!

Why must we go to school, dad?
Settle the question, do.
Tell us, dear daddy, as much as you can;
We're really relying on you.

To learn about fractions and Francis Drake,
I feel inclined to say,
And give your poor mother a bit of a break –
Now, push off and go out to play!

Why must we go to school, daddy?
Tell us, dear desperate dad.
One little hint, that's all we ask –
It's a puzzle that's driving us mad.

To find all the teachers something to do,
Or so I've heard it said,
And swot up the questions your kids'll ask you,
My darlings – now, buzz off to bed!

   Allan Ahlberg

Lost

Dear Mrs Butler, this is just a note
About our Raymond's coat
Which he came home without last night,
So I thought I'd better write.

He was minus his scarf as well, I regret
To say; and his grandma is most upset
As she knitted it and it's pure
Wool. You'll appreciate her feelings, I'm sure.

Also, his swimming towel has gone
Out of his P.E. bag, he says, and one
Of his socks, too – it's purplish and green
With a darn in the heel. His sister Jean

Has a pair very similar. And while
I remember, is there news yet of those Fair Isle
Gloves which Raymond lost that time
After the visit to the pantomime?

Well, I think that's all. I will close now.
Best wishes, yours sincerely, Maureen Howe
(Mrs). P.S. I did once write before
About his father's hat that Raymond wore

In the school play and later could not find,
But got no reply. Still, never mind,
Raymond tells me now he might have lost the note,
Or left it in the pocket of his coat.

Allan Ahlberg

The Coat

I patched my coat with sunlight.
It lasted for a day.
I patched my coat with moonlight,
But the lining came away.
I patched my coat with lightning
And it flew off in the storm.
I patched my coat with darkness:
That coat has kept me warm.

Dennis Lee

The Suit

Never thought much about fancy clothes
Until I bought myself a field.
It looks real good. Decent soil.
Plenty of room in which to grow.

I walk down the street now
And folks turn round and say, 'Hey,
There goes the feller who wears a field.'

Roger McGough

The Dunce

He says no with his head
but he says yes with his heart
he says yes to things he likes
he says no to the teacher
he is standing
he is being questioned
and all the problems are set
suddenly a gust of laughter shakes him
and he rubs out everything
the figures and the words
the dates and the names
the tests and the traps
and in spite of the schoolmaster
and the catcalls of the infant prodigies
with chalks of many colours
on the blackboard of sorrow
he draws the face of joy

Jacques Prévert

(*translated from the French by A. S. J. Tessimond*)

A Conversation Overheard

No school today?

Oh yes school everyday
we play games and
sing and dance and
say ABC and add and
pray and fight and
paint and cry and laugh.

Do you like school?

No.

Anonymous

Homework

Homework sits on top of Sunday, squashing Sunday flat.
Homework has the smell of Monday, homework's very fat.
Heavy books and piles of paper, answers I don't know.
Sunday evening's almost finished, now I'm going to go
Do my homework in the kitchen. Maybe just a snack,
Then I'll sit right down and start as soon as I run back
For some chocolate sandwich cookies. Then I'll really do
All that homework in a minute. First I'll see what new
Show they've got on television in the living room.
Everybody's laughing there, but misery and gloom
And a full refrigerator are where I am at.
I'll just have another sandwich. Homework's very fat.

Russell Hoban

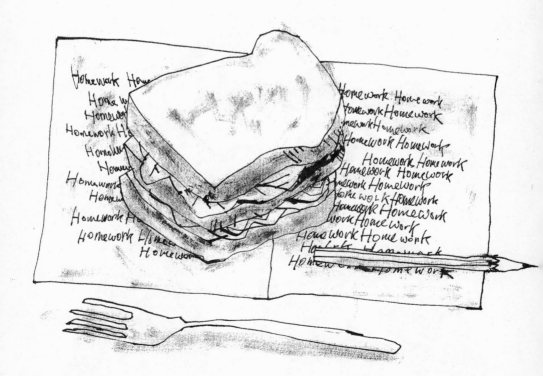

Playgrounds

Playgrounds are such gobby places.
Know what I mean?
Everyone seems to have something to
Talk about, giggle, whisper, scream and shout about,
I mean, it's like being in a parrot cage.

And playgrounds are such pushy places.
Know what I mean?
Everyone seems to have to
Run about, jump, kick, do cartwheels, handstands, fly
   around,
I mean, it's like being inside a whirlwind.

And playgrounds are such patchy places.
Know what I mean?
Everyone seems to
Go round in circles, lines and triangles, coloured shapes,
I mean, it's like being in a kaleidoscope.

And playgrounds are such pally places.
Know what I mean?
Everyone seems to
Have best friends, secrets, link arms, be in gangs.
Everyone, except me.

Know what I mean?

Berlie Doherty

Only the Wall

That first day
only the wall saw
the bully
trip the new boy
behind the shed,
and only the wall heard
the name he called,
a name that would stick
like toffee.

The second day
the wall didn't see
the fight
because too many
boys stood around,
but the wall heard
their cheers,
and no one cheered for
the new boy.

The third day
the wall felt
three bullies
lean against it,
ready to ambush
the new boy,
than the wall heard
thumps and cries,
and saw blood.

The fourth day
only the wall missed
the new boy
though five bullies
looked for him,
then picked another boy
instead. Next day
they had him back,
his face hit the wall.

The sixth day
only the wall knew
the bullies
would need that other boy
to savage.
The wall remembered
the new boy's face
going home,
saw he'd stay away.

Matthew Sweeney

The Bully

His head was a helmet
His muscles sprung steel
Each finger was
An electric eel
He was merciless
As the Bloody Tower
I was eight years old
And I was in his power

Adrian Mitchell

Stevie Scared

Stevie Scared, scared of the dark,
Scared of rats, of dogs that bark,
Scared of his fat dad, scared of his mother,
Scared of his sis and his tattooed brother,
Scared of tall girls, scared of boys,
Scared of ghosts and sudden noise,
Scared of spiders, scared of bees,
Scared of standing under trees,
Scared of shadows, scared of adders,
Scared of the devil, scared of ladders,
Scared of hailstones, scared of rain,
Scared of falling down the drain,
Stevie Scared, scared of showing
He's so scared and people knowing,
Spends his whole time kicking, fighting,
Shoving, pinching, butting, biting,
Bashing little kids about
(Just in case they find him out).

Richard Edwards

Lovesick

I'm scared of my own heart beat;
it's so loud someone might say
'who's on the drums?' and I'd blush
(not exactly beetroot) but blush
all the same.

I have these feelings.
I take them home from school
and tuck them up. In the morning
I say all the wrong things by accident
again and again.

Like, for instance, shouting *Miss*
in the middle of someone else saying
something. Usually Agnes MacNamara.
'In a minute,' says Miss. And I blush.
I hate MacNamara.

Miss is from Bangladesh and has
thick black hair, usually brushed
into one sleek pony. If I could tie the bow!
She has lovely eyes, dark pools.
Miss isn't married.

But I expect she will get married soon.
I think Mr Hudson wants to marry her.
Mr Hudson is always waiting in the corridor.
Him or that Agnes MacNamara.
Will I ever. Will I ever

Get older so that it doesn't hurt.
So that my heart doesn't hurt.
So that I don't spend all my time
with my fingers crossed and wishing:
Say something nice. Miss, Please. *Something*.

Jackie Kay

Yellow

*T*hink of something yellow.

The sun?
A fat ripe pear
or buttercup petals?

Yellow is butter.
Yellow is custard.
Yellow is yolks.

Yellow has all the answers.
Yellow is like
an advert that twists your eyes
till they light on yellow.

What is yellow?

Nobody answered.
Shakeela smiled
and stroked her yellow
shalwar khameez
so butterly
and buttercuply
that all our fingers turned yellow.

Helen Dunmore

Eily Kilbride

On the north side of Cork city
Where I sported and played
On the banks of my own lovely Lee
Having seen the goat break loose in Grand Parade

I met a child, Eily Kilbride
Who'd never heard of marmalade,
Whose experience of breakfast
Was coldly limited,

Whose entire school day
Was a bag of crisps,
Whose parents had no work to do,

Who went, once, in to the countryside,
Saw a horse with a feeding bag over its head
And thought it was sniffing glue.

Brendan Kennelly

The Janitor's Boy

Oh I'm in love with the janitor's boy,
  And the janitor's boy loves me;
He's going to hunt for a desert isle
  In our geography.

A desert isle with spicy trees
  Somewhere near Sheepshead Bay;
A right nice place, just fit for two
  Where we can live alway.

Oh I'm in love with the janitor's boy,
  He's busy as he can be;
And down in the cellar he's making a raft
  Out of an old settee.

He'll carry me off, I know that he will,
  For his hair is exceedingly red;
And the only thing that occurs to me
  Is to dutifully shiver in bed.

The day that we sail, I shall leave this brief note,
  For my parents I hate to annoy:
'I have flown away to an isle in the bay
  With the janitor's red-haired boy.'

Nathalia Crane

My Mother Said

My mother said, I never should
Play with gypsies in the wood.

If I did, then she would say:
'Naughty girl to disobey!

'Your hair shan't curl and your shoes shan't shine,
You gypsy girl, you shan't be mine!'

And my father said that if I did,
He'd rap my head with the teapot-lid.

My mother said that I never should
Play with the gypsies in the wood.

The wood was dark, the grass was green;
By came Sally with a tambourine.

I went to sea – no ship to get across;
I paid ten shillings for a blind white horse.

I upped on his back and was off in a crack,
Sally tell my mother I shall never come back.

Anonymous

Dear Mum,

while you were out
a cup went and broke itself,
a crack appeared in the blue vase
your great-great grandad
brought back from Mr Ming in China.
Somehow, without me even turning on the tap,
the sink mysteriously overflowed.
A strange jam-stain,
about the size of a boy's hand,
appeared on the kitchen wall.
I don't think we will ever discover
exactly how the cat
managed to turn on the washing-machine
(specially from the inside),
or how Sis's pet rabbit went and mistook
the waste-disposal unit for a burrow.
I can tell you I was scared when,
as if by magic,
a series of muddy footprints
appeared on the new white carpet.
I was being good
(honest)
but I think the house is haunted so,
knowing you're going to have a fit,
I've gone over to Gran's for a bit.

Brian Patten

Cat in the Tumble Drier

Oh Oh Oh
the drier's on the go
can't get out and
try to shout and
mouth full of fluff and
other stuff and
scrambling paws and
tea towel in my jaws and
vest round my tail and
start to wail and
tail round my ear and
drier up a gear and
ear caught up in claw and
see you through the door and
flannel round my leg and
I start to beg and
fur hot and frizzy and
head's gone sizzle dizzy and
you're there through the glass and
more hankies whizz past and
Oh Oh Oh
the drier starts to slow
my fur starts to spark and
the pillow-cases bark and
the nightdress winks and
the clean wash sinks
to a stop

Jo Shapcott

Woman Work

I've got the children to tend
The clothes to mend
The floor to mop
The food to shop
Then the chicken to fry
The baby to dry
I got company to feed
The garden to weed
I've got the shirts to press
The tots to dress
The cane to be cut
I gotta clean up this hut
Then see about the sick
And the cotton to pick.

Shine on me, sunshine
Rain on me, rain
Fall softly, dewdrops
And cool my brow again.

Storm, blow me from here
With your fiercest wind
Let me float across the sky
'Til I can rest again.

Fall gently, snowflakes
Cover me with white
Cold icy kisses and
Let me rest tonight.

Sun, rain, curving sky
Mountain, oceans, leaf and stone
Star shine, moon glow
You're all that I can call my own.

Maya Angelou

Lady-bird, Lady-bird

Lady-bird, lady-bird,
　Fly away home,
Your house is on fire,
　Your children all gone.
Lady-bird, lady-bird,
　Lost and alone,
No family to care for,
　No work to be done.

Anonymous

The True History of Resurrection Jack

Resurrection Jack lay under a stone
curled like a grub and quite alone
he was three weeks old and his skin was black
and he didn't even know that his name was Jack

Bare was the veldt and hard as bone
where he lay beneath his burying-stone
ditched by a mother who grudged him breath
but that little baby gave the slip to death

White folk passing heard a sound
thought it was coming out of the ground
paused to listen and heard a moan
tracked poor Jack and rolled that stone

Raised him up in the eye of the sun
and that was the day when his life begun
he went with the white folk and never looked back
and they grew together though his skin was black

He lived long years till his life was done
with the folk who'd lifted him into the sun
for there's things go deeper than white or black

and that's the true tale of Resurrection Jack.

Evangeline Paterson

St Brigid and the Baker

As Brigid was walking
the old narrow track
she passed by a baker
with bread in his sack.

She put out a hand
from the fold of her cloak
and these are the words
she softly spoke:

'*Please give me a loaf
for my sisters and me,
and we'll share it tonight
as we sit to our tea.*'

But the baker, he muttered
and shook a mean head.
'*If you want to eat, sister,
then bake your own bread.*'

She looked in his eyes then,
but all that she found
was a stare that was hard
as the stones on the ground.

So Brigid passed quietly
along the hard track
as the bread turned to stone
on the baker's back.

Tony Mitton

Ballad of the Bread Man

Mary stood in the kitchen
  Baking a loaf of bread.
An angel flew in through the window.
  'We've a job for you,' he said.

'God in his big gold heaven,
  Sitting in his big blue chair,
Wanted a mother for his little son.
  Suddenly saw you there.'

Mary shook and trembled,
  'It isn't true what you say.'
'Don't say that,' said the angel.
  'The baby's on its way.'

Joseph was in the workshop
  Planing a piece of wood.
'The old man's past it,' the neighbours said.
  'That girl's been up to no good.'

'And who was that elegant fellow,'
  They said, 'in the shiny gear?'
The things they said about Gabriel
  Were hardly fit to hear.

Mary never answered,
  Mary never replied.
She kept the information,
  Like the baby, safe inside.

It was election winter.
   They went to vote in town.
When Mary found her time had come
   The hotels let her down.

The baby was born in an annexe
   Next to the local pub.
At midnight, a delegation
   Turned up from the Farmers' Club.

They talked about an explosion
   That made a hole in the sky,
Said they'd been sent to the Lamb & Flag
   To see God come down from on high.

A few days later a bishop
   And a five-star general were seen
With the head of an African country
   In a bullet-proof limousine.

'We've come,' they said, 'with tokens
   For the little boy to choose.'
Told the tale about war and peace
   In the television news.

After them came the soldiers
   With rifle and bomb and gun,
Looking for enemies of the state.
   The family had packed and gone.

When they got back to the village
   The neighbours said, to a man,
'That boy will never be one of us,
   Though he does what he blessed well can.'

He went round to all the people
  A paper crown on his head.
Here is some bread from my father.
  Take, eat, he said.

Nobody seemed very hungry.
  Nobody seemed to care.
Nobody saw the god in himself
  Quietly standing there.

He finished up in the papers.
  He came to a very bad end.
He was charged with bringing the living to life.
  No man was that prisoner's friend,

There's only one kind of punishment
  To fit that kind of crime.
They rigged a trial and shot him dead,
  They were only just in time,

They lifted the young man by the leg,
  They lifted him by the arm,
They locked him in a cathedral
  In case he came to harm.

They stored him safe as water
  Under seven rocks.
One Sunday morning he burst out
  Like a jack-in-the-box.

Through the town he went walking.
  He showed them the holes in his head.
Now do you want any loaves? he cried.
  'Not today,' they said.

Charles Causley

People

I like people quite well
at a little distance.
I like to see them passing and passing
and going their own way,
especially if I see their aloneness alive in them.
Yet I don't want them to come near.
If they will only leave me alone
I can still have the illusion that there is room enough in the
    world.

D. H. Lawrence

The Sound Collector

A stranger called this morning
Dressed all in black and grey
Put every sound into a bag
And carried them away

The whistling of the kettle
The turning of the lock
The purring of the kitten
The ticking of the clock

The popping of the toaster
The crunching of the flakes
When you spread the marmalade
The scraping noise it makes

The hissing of the frying-pan
The ticking of the grill
The bubbling of the bathtub
As it starts to fill

The drumming of the raindrops
On the window-pane
When you do the washing-up
The gurgle of the drain

The crying of the baby
The squeaking of the chair
The swishing of the curtain
The creaking of the stair

A stranger called this morning
He didn't leave his name
Left us only silence
Life will never be the same.

Roger McGough

Counting the Mad

This one was put in a jacket,
This one was sent home,
This one was given bread and meat
But would eat none,
And this one cried No No No No
All day long.

This one looked at the window
As though it were a wall,
This one saw things that were not there,
This one things that were,
And this one cried No No No No
All day long.

This one thought himself a bird,
This one a dog,
And this one thought himself a man,
An ordinary man,
And cried and cried No No No No
All day long.

Donald Justice

The Nobody on the Hill

No one knows he lives there,
not even the postman
as nobody writes.
His family, if he had any,
are dead, and years before
they thought him dead
for certain. They'd laugh
if they saw him on this hill.

They'd stand before his hut
and shake their heads.
Home in the city
they had a grand house,
and he lived there once.
An avenue of trees
instead of this hill.
Even their ghosts avoid it.

Beyond the hill is a bog
and beyond that, nothing –
this suits him. He hunted
long and far for the site.
He hammered together the hut
in two days. He never leaves
the hill. He'll die there
and no one will find him.

Matthew Sweeney

The Hermit

What moves that lonely man is not the boom
  Of waves that break against the cliff so strong;
Nor roar of thunder, when that travelling voice
  Is caught by rocks that carry far along.

'Tis not the groan of oak tree in its prime,
  When lightning strikes its solid heart to dust;
Nor frozen pond when, melted by the sun,
  It suddenly doth break its sparkling crust.

What moves that man is when the blind bat taps
  His window when he sits alone at night;
Or when the small bird sounds like some great beast
  Among the dead, dry leaves so frail and light.

Or when the moths on his night-pillow beat
  Such heavy blows he fears they'll break his bones;
Or when a mouse inside the papered walls,
  Comes like a tiger crunching through the stones.

W. H. Davies

At a Country Fair

At a bygone Western country fair
I saw a giant led by a dwarf
With a red string like a long thin scarf;
How much he was the stronger there
   The giant seemed unaware.

And then I saw that the giant was blind,
And the dwarf a shrewd-eyed little thing;
The giant, mild, timid, obeyed the string
As if he had no independent mind,
   Or will of any kind.

Wherever the dwarf decided to go
At his heels the other trotted meekly,
(Perhaps – I know not – reproaching weakly)
Like one Fate bade that it must be so,
   Whether he wished or no.

Various sights in various climes
I have seen, and more I may see yet,
But that sight never shall I forget,
And have thought it the sorriest of pantomimes,
   If once, a hundred times!

Thomas Hardy

The Blind Boxer

He goes with basket, and slow feet,
To sell his nuts from street to street;
The very terror of his kind,
Till blackened eyes had made him blind.
Aye, this is Boxer Bob, the man
That had hard muscles harder than
A schoolboy's bones; who held his ground
When six tall bullies sparred around.
Small children now, that have no grace,
Can steal his nuts before his face;
And, when he threatens with his hands,
Mock him two feet from where he stands;
Mock him who could, some years ago,
Have leapt five feet to strike a blow.
Poor Bobby, I remember when
Thou wert a god to drunken men;
But now they push thee off, or crack
Thy nuts and give no money back;
They swear they'll strike thee in the face,
Dost thou not hurry from that place;
Such are the men that once would pay
To keep thee drunk from day to day.
With all thy strength and cunning skill,
Thy courage, lasting breath, and will,
Thou'rt helpless now; a little ball,
No bigger than a cherry small,
Has now refused to guide and lead
Twelve stone of strong, hard flesh that need
But that ball's light to make thee leap

And strike these cowards down like sheep.
Poor, helpless Bobby, blind: I see
Thy working face and pity thee.

W. H. Davies

My Mother Saw a Dancing Bear

My mother saw a dancing bear
By the schoolyard, a day in June.
The keeper stood with chain and bar
And whistle-pipe, and played a tune.

And bruin lifted up its head
And lifted up its dusty feet,
And all the children laughed to see
It caper in the summer heat.

They watched as for the Queen it died.
They watched it march. They watched it halt.
They heard the keeper as he cried,
'Now, roly-poly!' 'Somersault!'

And then, my mother said, there came
The keeper with a begging-cup,
The bear with burning coat of fur,
Shaming the laughter to a stop.

They paid a penny for the dance,
But what they saw was not the show;
Only, in bruin's aching eyes,
Far-distant forests, and the snow.

Charles Causley

The Small Brown Bear

The small brown bear
fishes
with stony paws

eating ice salmon
all waterfall slippery
till his teeth ache.

Michael Baldwin

Panda Power

'Give me bamboo shoots.' My panda's run amuck.
He's tearing up my bedroom; the family's panic-struck.

'Make my day with those shoots – I want that foliage.'
He's turned the kitchen over; my dad's behind the fridge.

'Shoots or I torch the house.' I can smell his bamboo breath:
He's prowling round the bathroom. My brother's scared to
    death.

'Bamboo shoots or you're dead.' He's toting a big gun.
He's rooting round the garden, he's kidnapped my poor
    mum.

'Sing!' I shout to the family. 'Sing him a lullaby.'
They're gobsmacked, but they do it: 'Close your pretty eye,'

Etcetera – and it's working; he's snoring little snores.
I give him a big cuddle and carry him indoors.

By now he's fast asleep in his rumpled gangster suit,
and I leave him chewing on an imaginary bamboo shoot.

Jo Shapcott

The Tyger

Tyger Tyger, burning bright,
In the forests of the night;
What immortal hand or eye,
Could frame thy fearful symmetry?

In what distant deeps or skies,
Burnt the fire of thine eyes?
On what wings dare he aspire?
What the hand, dare sieze the fire?

And what shoulder, and what art,
Could twist the sinews of thy heart?
And when thy heart began to beat,
What dread hand? and what dread feet?

What the hammer? what the chain,
In what furnace was thy brain?
What the anvil? what dread grasp,
Dare its deadly terrors clasp?

When the stars threw down their spears
And water'd heaven with their tears;
Did he smile his work to see?
Did he who made the Lamb make thee?

Tyger Tyger burning bright,
In the forests of the night:
What immortal hand or eye,
Dare frame thy fearful symmetry?

William Blake

The King of Cats Sends a Postcard to His Wife

Keep your whiskers crisp and clean.
Do not let the mice grow lean.
Do not let yourself grow fat
like a common kitchen cat.

Have you set the kittens free?
Do they sometimes ask for me?
Is our catnip growing tall?
Did you patch the garden wall?

Clouds are gentle walls that hide
gardens on the other side.
Tell the tabby cats I take
all my meals with William Blake,

lunch at noon and tea at four,
served in splendour on the shore
at the tinkling of a bell.
Tell them I am sleeping well.

Tell them I have come so far,
brought by Blake's celestial car,
buffeted by wind and rain,
I may not get home again.

Take this message to my friends.
Say the King of Catnip sends
to the cat who winds his clocks
a thousand sunsets in a box,

to the cat who brings the ice
the shadows of a dozen mice
(serve them with assorted dips
and eat them like potato chips),

and to the cat who guards his door
a net for catching stars, and more
(if with patience he abide):
catnip from the other side.

Nancy Willard

Cat's Funeral

Bury her deep, down deep,
Safe in the earth's cold keep,
    Bury her deep –

No more to watch bird stir;
No more to clean dark fur;
No more to glisten as silk;
No more to revel in milk;
    No more to purr.

Bury her deep, down deep;
She is beyond warm sleep.
She will not walk in the night;
She will not wake to the light.
    Bury her deep.

E. V. Rieu

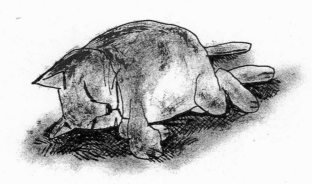

Cleaning Ladies

Belly stuffed with dust and fluff,
  The hoover moos and drones,
Grazing down on the carpet pasture:
  Cow with electric bones.

Up in the tree of a chair the cat
  Switches off its purr,
Stretches, blinks: a neat pink tongue
  Vacuum-cleans its fur.

  Kit Wright

Be Like the Bird

Be like the bird, who
Resting in his flight
On a twig too slight
Feels it bend beneath him,
Yet sings
Knowing he has wings.

Victor Hugo

Riddle*

His flat face may look like a light switch
and
his eyes like a pair of saucers
and
his beak like tiny tin-snips
and
his body like a soft pellet
but
to who?

George Szirtes

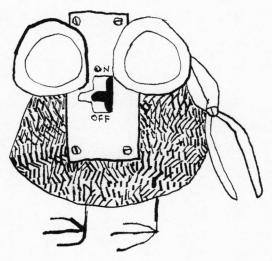

*Owl

Starling on a Green Lawn

He makes such a business of going somewhere
he's like a hopping with a bird in it.

The somewhere's an any place, which he recognises at once.
His track is zig – zag zig zag – zag.

He angles himself to the sun and his blackness
becomes something fallen from a stained-glass window.

He's a guy King, a guy Prince, though his only royal habit
is to walk with his hands clasped behind his back.

Now he's flown up like a mad glove on to a fence post.
He squinnies at the world and draws a cork from a bottle.

Norman MacCaig

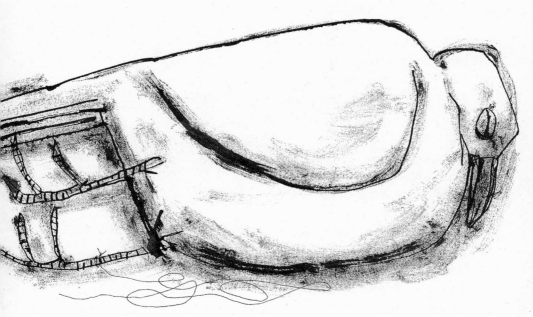

Song

I had a dove and the sweet dove died;
   And I have thought it died of grieving:
O, what could it grieve for? it was tied,
   With a silken thread of my own hand's weaving;
Sweet little red feet! why did you die –
Why would you leave me, sweet dove! why?
   You liv'd alone on the forest-tree,
Why, pretty thing! could you not live with me?
I kiss'd you oft and gave you white peas;
Why not live sweetly, as in the green trees?

John Keats

Song of the Snails Who Go to the Funeral

Two snails are setting out
For the funeral of a leaf
The shells they wear are black
They've crêpe tied round their horns
They are setting out in the darkness
Of a very fine autumn evening
But alas when they arrive
It is already Spring
And so the dry dead leaves
Are all alive again
And the two black solemn snails
Are very disappointed
But look there is the sun
The sun that says to them
Come make yourselves at home
Come friends please take a seat
And take a glass of beer
And if you're so inclined
Come take the Paris bus
It starts at eight this evening
You'll see the countryside
But don't don't mourn my friends
Come take this tip from me
Black doesn't suit the complexion
It's dreadfully unbecoming
This talk of shrouds and coffins
Is terribly depressing
Dear friends be your natural colour
The natural colour of life
And then the whole concourse of animals
And trees and flowers and plants

Suddenly start to sing
To sing for all they're worth
To sing the song of life
To sing the song of summer
And everyone starts drinking
Drinking each other's health
And the evening's a wonderful evening
A wonderful summer evening
And at last the two black snails
Decided to start for home
They go off full of emotion
They go off full of happiness
And having had plenty to drink
They're a little unsteady on their feet
But high in the sky the moon
The watching moon protects them

Jacques Prévert

(*translated from the French by A. S. J. Tessimond*)

Worms and the Wind

Worms would rather be worms.
Ask a worm and he says, 'Who knows what a worm
   knows?'
Worms go down and up and over and under.
Worms like tunnels.
When worms talk they talk about the worm world.
Worms like it in the dark.
Neither the sun nor the moon interests a worm.
Zigzag worms hate circle worms.
Curve worms never trust square worms.
Worms know what worms want.
Slide worms are suspicious of crawl worms.
One worm asks another, 'How does your belly drag today?'
The shape of a crooked worm satisfies a crooked worm.
A straight worm says, 'Why not be straight?'
Worms tired of crawling begin to slither.
Long worms slither farther than short worms.
Middle-sized worms say, 'It is nice to be neither long nor
   short.'
Old worms teach young worms to say, 'Don't be sorry for
   me unless you have been a worm and lived in worm
   places and read worm books.'
When worms go to war they dig in, come out and fight, dig
   in again, come out and fight again, dig in again, and so
   on.
Worms underground never hear the wind overground and
   sometimes they ask, 'What is this wind we hear of?'

Carl Sandburg

The Tickle Rhyme

'Who's that tickling my back?' said the wall.
'Me,' said a small
Caterpillar. 'I'm learning
To crawl.'

Ian Serraillier

H25

Hedgehogs hog the hedges,
roadhogs hog the roads
I'd like to build a motorway
for badgers, frogs and toads.

With halts for hungry hedgehogs
at an all-night service station;
four lanes wide and free from man
right across the nation.

Free from oil and petrol fumes,
and free from motor cars,
to see the busy hedgehogs trot
underneath the stars.

Adrian Henri

At the Bottom of the Garden

No, it isn't an old football
grown all shrunken and prickly
because it was left out so long
at the bottom of the garden.

It's only Hedgehog
who, when she thinks I'm not looking,
unballs herself to move –
Like bristling black lightning.

Grace Nichols

Black dot

a black dot
a jelly tot

a scum-nail
a jiggle-tail

a cool kicker
a sitting slicker

a panting puffer
a fly-snuffer

a high hopper
a belly-flopper

a catalogue
     to make me
        frog

Libby Houston

Mice Are Funny Little Creatures

Mice are funny little creatures
                                        you nearly don't see them
Getting out so fast under the sacks more like a bird's shadow
Amazing living like that on fearful lightning
Funny too how they smell like lions did you ever smell lions
    in a zoo?
You see one come tottering out
When maybe you're just sitting quiet and he'll come right
    out
With his nose-end wriggling investigating
Every speck of air he seems to be – high on his trembly legs
Very long legs really and his queer little pink hands
Little monkey's hands very human I always think
And his wiry bent tail high up there behind him
Wavering about he looks to be on a tight-rope

Then he finds something and starts trembling over it
His nibbling is an all over trembling, his whole body
Trembles as if he were starving and couldn't wait
But it's really listening, he's listening for danger – so
    sensitive
He's trembling it's like a tenderness
So many things can hurt him
And his ears thin as warm wax you've squeezed between
    your finger and thumb
Always remind me of an elephant's ears
A bit shapeless and his long face really like an elephant
If he had a trunk he'd be a tiny elephant exact
At least his face would and his tail being a kind of trunk at
    the wrong end
And his feet being so opposite to great elephant's feet
Help remind you of elephants altogether he really is like an
    elephant

Except his size of course but that reminds you of elephants
    too
Because it's the opposite end of the animals
Like they say extremes meet I can understand
Why mice frighten elephants but they're dear little things
I don't mind what they nibble

Ted Hughes

The Bat

By day the bat is cousin to the mouse;
He likes the attic of an aging house.

His fingers make a hat about his head.
His pulse-beat is so slow we think him dead.

He loops in crazy figures half the night
Among the trees that face the corner light.

But when he brushes up against a screen,
We are afraid of what our eyes have seen:

For something is amiss or out of place
When mice with wings can wear a human face.

Theodore Roethke

'Observe this precept whenever you can'

Observe this precept whenever you can –
Never make friends with an elephant-man;
For an elephant-man has a pet to keep,
Eating and drinking, awake or asleep,
And if you are friendly one day you'll see,
When the elephant-keeper comes to tea,
That, not in the least by chance or whim,
The elephant will accompany him.
Then as soon as the animal's through the door
You'll notice cracks in the parlour floor,
And however much you may frown or stare
He'll sit across-legged on an easy chair,
And swill your tea with his cumbrous trunk
Till you think 'My Word, what a lot he's drunk.'
And if you should offer a mild reproof
He'll be up from your table and off with your roof …
In your sorrows you'll only sink deeper and deeper
If you ever make friends with an elephant-keeper.

Sa'di

(*translated from the Persian*)

Elephant Dreams

1   I'm so small
I can crawl
under a leaf

and I can look
into the world
from underneath.

2   There's a huge grey cloud in the sky.
It's me.
I float down on to a sycamore
tree.
I burst like a bag and the rain falls
out.
I swim in my rain like a huge grey
trout.

3   My
long
trunk
goes
round
the
world
twice!

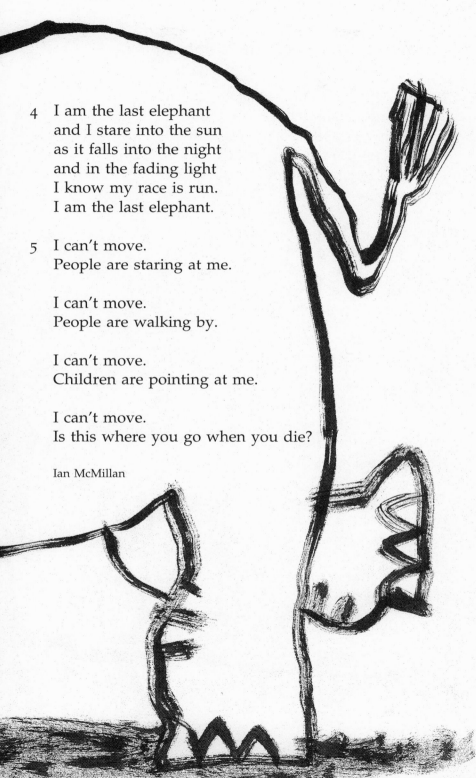

4   I am the last elephant
    and I stare into the sun
    as it falls into the night
    and in the fading light
    I know my race is run.
    I am the last elephant.

5   I can't move.
    People are staring at me.

    I can't move.
    People are walking by.

    I can't move.
    Children are pointing at me.

    I can't move.
    Is this where you go when you die?

    Ian McMillan

The Blind Men and the Elephant

It was six men of Hindostan,
To learning much inclined,
Who went to see the elephant,
(Though all of them were blind):
That each by observation
Might satisfy his mind.

The first approached the elephant,
And happening to fall
Against his broad and sturdy side,
At once began to bawl,
'Bless me, it seems the elephant
Is very like a wall.'

The second, feeling of his tusk,
Cried, 'Ho! what have we here
So very round and smooth and sharp?
To me 'tis mighty clear
This wonder of an elephant
Is very like a spear.'

The third approached the animal,
And happening to take
The squirming trunk within his hands,
Then boldly up and spake;
'I see,' quoth he, 'the elephant
Is very like a snake.'

The fourth stretched out his eager hand
And felt about the knee,
'What most this mighty beast is like
Is mighty plain,' quoth he;
' 'Tis clear enough the elephant
Is very like a tree.'

The fifth who chanced to touch the ear
Said, 'Even the blindest man
Can tell what this resembles most;
Deny the fact who can,
This marvel of an elephant
Is very like a fan.'

The sixth no sooner had begun
About the beast to grope
Than, seizing on the swinging tail
That fell within his scope,
'I see,' cried he, 'the elephant
Is very like a rope.'

And so these men of Hindostan
Disputed loud and long,
Each of his own opinion
Exceeding stiff and strong,
Though each was partly in the right,
And all were in the wrong!

John Godfrey Saxe

Down Behind the Dustbin

Down behind the dustbin
I met a dog called Ted.
'Leave me alone,' he says,
'I'm just going to bed.'

Down behind the dustbin
I met a dog called Felicity.
'It's a bit dark here,' she said,
'They've cut off the electricity.'

Down behind the dustbin
I met a dog called Roger.
'Do you own this bin?' I said.
'No. I'm only the lodger.'

Ian said,
Down behind the dustbin
I met a dog called Sue.
'What are you doing here?' I said.
'I've got nothing else to do.'

Down behind the dustbin
I met a dog called Anne.
'I'm just off now,' she said,
'to see a dog about a man.'

Down behind the dustbin
I met a dog called Jack.
'Are you going anywhere?' I said.
'No. I'm just coming back.'

Down behind the dustbin
I met a dog called Billy.
'I'm not talking to you,' I said,
'if you're going to be silly.'

Down behind the dustbin
I met a dog called Barry.
He tried to take the bin away
but it was too heavy to carry.

Down behind the dustbin
I met a dog called Mary.
'I wish I wasn't a dog,' she said,
'I wish I was a canary.'

Michael Rosen

Jabberwocky

'Twas brillig, and the slithy toves
Did gyre and gimble in the wabe;
All mimsy were the borogroves,
And the mome raths outgrabe.

Beware the Jabberwock, my son!
The jaws that bite, the claws that catch!
Beware the Jubjub bird and shun
The frumious Bandersnatch!

He took his vorpal sword in hand:
Long time the manxome foe he sought –
So rested he by the Tumtum tree,
And stood awhile in thought.

And as in uffish thought he stood,
The Jabberwock, with eyes of flame,
Came whiffling through the tulgey wood,
And burbled as it came!

One two! One two! and through and through
The vorpal blade went snicker-snack!
He left it dead, and with its head
He went galumphing back.

'And hast thou slain the Jabberwock!
Come to my arms, my beamish boy!
O frabjous day! Callooh! Callay!'
He chortled in his joy.

'Twas brillig, and the slithy toves
Did gyre and gimble in the wabe;
All mimsy were the borogoves,
And the mome raths outgrabe.

Lewis Carroll

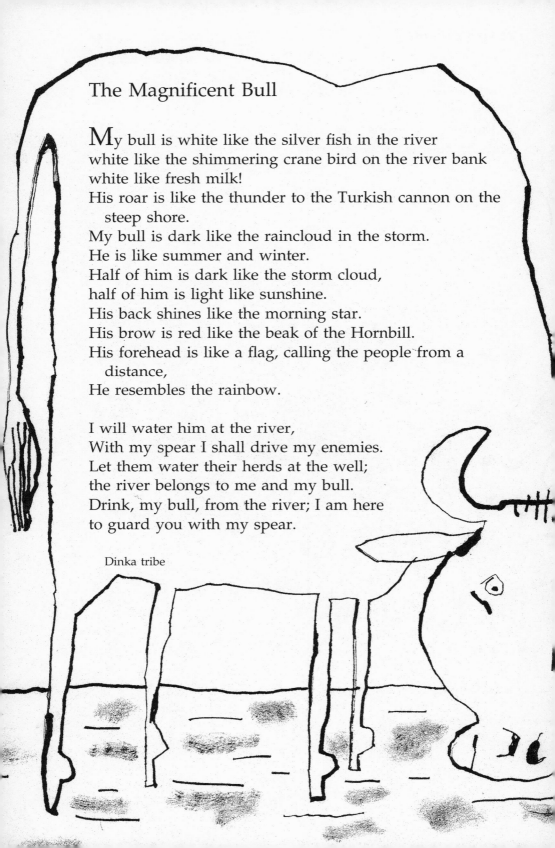

The Magnificent Bull

My bull is white like the silver fish in the river
white like the shimmering crane bird on the river bank
white like fresh milk!
His roar is like the thunder to the Turkish cannon on the
   steep shore.
My bull is dark like the raincloud in the storm.
He is like summer and winter.
Half of him is dark like the storm cloud,
half of him is light like sunshine.
His back shines like the morning star.
His brow is red like the beak of the Hornbill.
His forehead is like a flag, calling the people from a
   distance,
He resembles the rainbow.

I will water him at the river,
With my spear I shall drive my enemies.
Let them water their herds at the well;
the river belongs to me and my bull.
Drink, my bull, from the river; I am here
to guard you with my spear.

Dinka tribe

My Twelve Oxen

With hay, with how, with hoy!
Sawest thou not my oxen, thou little pretty boy?

I have twelve oxen that be fair and brown,
and they go a-grazing down by the town.

I have twelve oxen, and they be fair and white,
and they go a-grazing down by the dyke.

I have twelve oxen, and they be fair and black,
and they go a-grazing down by the lake.

I have twelve oxen, and they be fair and red,
and they go a-grazing down by the mead.

Anonymous

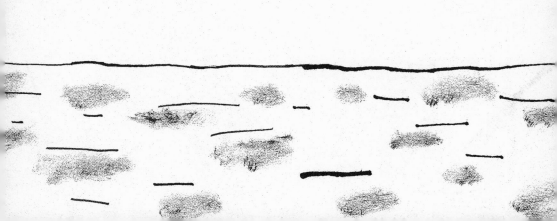

The Sea

They wash their hands in it.
The salt turns to soap
In their hands. Wearing it
At their wrists, they make bracelets
Of it; it runs in beads
On their jackets. A child's
Plaything? It has hard whips
That it cracks, and knuckles
To pummel you. It scrubs
And scours; it chews rocks
To sand; its embraces
Leave you without breath. Mostly
It is a stomach, where bones,
Wrecks, continents are digested.

R. S. Thomas

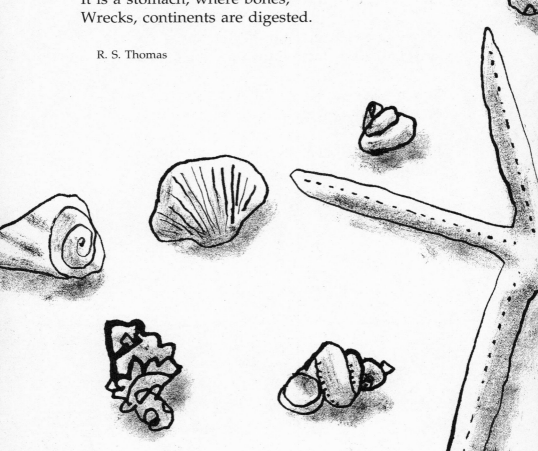

maggie and milly and molly and may

maggie and milly and molly and may
went down to the beach(to play one day)

and maggie discovered a shell that sang
so sweetly she couldn't remember her troubles,and

milly befriended a stranded star
whose rays five languid fingers were;

and molly was chased by a horrible thing
which raced sideways while blowing bubbles:and

may came home with a smooth round stone
as small as a world and as large as alone.

For whatever we lose(like a you or a me)
it's always ourselves we find in the sea

E. E. Cummings

Thoughts like an Ocean

The sea comes to me on the shore
On lacy slippered feet
And shyly, slyly slides away
With a murmur of defeat.

And as I stand there wondering
Strange thoughts spin round my head
Of why and where and what and when
And if not, why, what then?

Where do lobsters come from?
And where anemones?
And are there other worlds out there
With other mysteries?

Why do *I* walk upon dry land
While fishes haunt the sea?
And as I think about their lives
Do they too think of me?

Why is water, water?
Why does it wet my hand?
Are there really as many stars
As there are grains of sand?

And where would the ocean go to
If there were no gravity?
And where was I before I lived?
And where's eternity?

Perhaps the beach I'm standing on
Perhaps this stretch of sand
Perhaps the Universe itself
Lies on someone else's hand?

And isn't it strange how this water and I
At this moment happened to meet
And how this tide sweeps half the world
Before stopping at my feet.

Gareth Owen

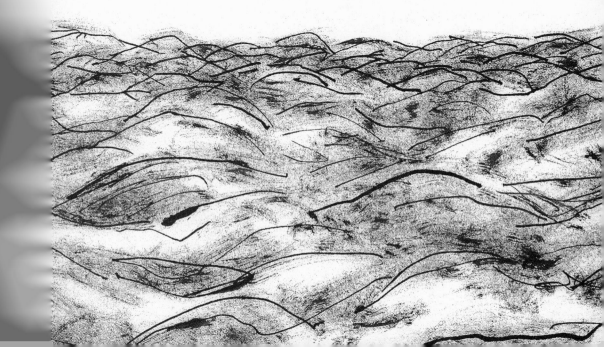

Advice to Young Children

'Children who paddle where the ocean bed shelves steeply
Must take great care they do not
Paddle too deeply.'

Thus spake the awful aging couple
Whose heart the years had turned to rubble.

But the little children, to save any bother,
Let it in at one ear and out at the other.

Stevie Smith

Neither Out Far nor In Deep

The people along the sand
All turn and look one way.
They turn their back on the land.
They look at the sea all day.

As long as it takes to pass
A ship keeps raising its hull;
The wetter ground like glass
Reflects a standing gull.

The land may vary more;
But wherever the truth may be –
The water comes ashore,
And the people look at the sea.

They cannot look out far.
They cannot look in deep.
But when was that ever a bar
To any watch they keep?

Robert Frost

Not Waving but Drowning

Nobody heard him, the dead man,
But still he lay moaning:
I was much further out than you thought
And not waving but drowning.

Poor chap, he always loved larking
And now he's dead.
It must have been too cold for him his heart gave way,
They said.

Oh, no no no, it was too cold always
(Still the dead one lay moaning)
I was much too far out all my life
And not waving but drowning.

Stevie Smith

Sea Fever

I must down to the seas again, to the lonely sea and the sky,
And all I ask is a tall ship and a star to steer her by,
And the wheel's kick and the wind's song and the white
    sail's shaking,
And a grey mist on the sea's face and a grey dawn breaking.

I must down to the seas again, for the call of the running
    tide
Is a wild call and a clear call that may not be denied;
And all I ask is a windy day with the white clouds flying,
And the flung spray and the blown spume, and the seagulls
    crying.

I must down to the seas again, to the vagrant gypsy life,
To the gull's way and the whale's way where the wind's
    like a whetted knife;
And all I ask is a merry yarn from a laughing fellow-rover,
And quiet sleep and a sweet dream when the long trick's
    over.

John Masefield

A Smuggler's Song

If you wake at midnight, and hear a horse's feet,
Don't go drawing back the blind, or looking in the street,
Them that asks no questions isn't told a lie.
Watch the wall, my darling, while the Gentlemen go by!
   Five-and-twenty ponies
   Trotting through the dark –
   Brandy for the Parson,
   'Baccy for the Clerk;
   Laces for a lady, letters for a spy,
And watch the wall, my darling, while the Gentlemen go by!

Running round the woodlump if you chance to find
Little barrels, roped and tarred, all full of brandy-wine,
Don't you shout to come and look, nor use 'em for your play.
Put the brushwood back again – and they'll be gone next
   day!

If you see the stable-door setting open wide;
If you see a tired horse lying down inside;
If your mother mends a coat cut about and tore;
If the lining's wet and warm – don't you ask no more!

If you meet King George's men, dressed in blue and red,
You be careful what you say, and mindful what is said.
If they call you 'pretty maid', and chuck you 'neath the chin,
Don't you tell where no one is, nor yet where no one's been!

Knocks and footsteps round the house – whistles after dark –
You've no call for running out till the house-dogs bark.
Trusty's here, and Pincher's here, and see how dumb they
   lie –
They don't fret to follow when the Gentlemen go by!

If you do as you've been told, 'likely there's a chance,
You'll be given a dainty doll, all the way from France,
With a cap of Valenciennes, and a velvet hood –
A present from the Gentlemen, along o' being good!
   Five-and-twenty ponies
   Trotting through the dark –
   Brandy for the Parson,
   'Baccy for the Clerk.
Them that asks no questions isn't told a lie –
Watch the wall, my darling, while the Gentlemen go by!

   Rudyard Kipling

Going to America

With sea-blue hats and sea-blue socks,
   Going to America,
We set sail in a cardboard box,
   Going to America,
The waves reared up and hid the sky,
   Going to America,
And sharks, as keen as knives, slid by,
   Going to America,
We rode the storm, we raced the gale,
   Going to America,
When, suddenly, up bulged a whale,
   Going to America,
The whale's tail slapped our skin-thin ship,
   Going to America,
And stove us in, and through the rip,
   Going to America,
Poured streaming seas, gushed freezing waves,
   Going to America,
Threatening us with watery graves,
   Going to America,
Land-ho! A wild coast loomed ahead,
   Going to America,
'Swim for your lives!' the Captain said,
   Going to America,
We dived, we swam, we fought our way,
   Going to America,
To the foot of a sheer cliff veiled in spray,
   Going to America,
And clinging on with teeth and nails,
   Going to America,
We climbed that cliff to search for sails,
   Going to America,

And when at last we reached the top,
   Going to America,
And balanced there, a voice cried, 'Stop!
How many times have I told you
Not to climb on the back of the sofa!'

   Richard Edwards

O Sailor, Come Ashore

O Sailor, come ashore,
   What have you brought for me?
Red coral, white coral,
   Coral from the sea.

I did not dig it from the ground,
   Nor pluck it from a tree;
Feeble insects made it
   In the stormy sea.

   Christina Rossetti

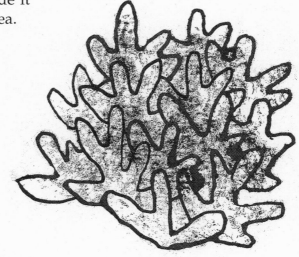

Look, No Hands

Without muscles, without an arm or hand grip,
look how I wind bend back trees' big limbs.

Without wheels, without a down-hill,
look how I the sea roll and roll along.

Without a hurt, without a bruise,
look how I waterfall tumble down rocks.

Without bricks, without hammer or nails,
look how I tree build a house for birds.

Without apprenticeship, without D.I.Y. store,
look how I eagle build my family's nest.

Without getting even one single penny,
look how we apple trees give up our red apples.

Without a hose, without a sprinkler,
look how I sky water gardens with my rain.

James Berry

New Year exhilaration

On the third day
Finds its proper weather. Pressure
Climbing and the hard blue sky
Scoured by gales. The world's being
Swept clean. Twigs that can't cling
Go flying, last leaves ripped off
Bowl along roads like daring mice. Imagine
The new moon hightide sea under this
Rolling of air-weights. Exhilaration
Lashes everything. Windows flash,
White houses dazzle, fields glow red.
Seas pour in over the land, invisible maelstroms
Set the house-joints creaking. Every twig-end
Writes its circles and the earth
Is massaged with roots. The powers of hills
Hold their bright faces in the wind-shine.
The hills are being honed. The river
Thunders like a factory, its weirs
Are tremendous engines. People
Walk precariously, the whole landscape
Is imperilled, like a tarpaulin
With the wind under it. 'It nearly
Blew me up the chymbley!' And a laugh
Blows away like a hat.

(3 January 1975)

Ted Hughes

Wet Evening in April

The birds sang in the wet trees
And as I listened to them it was a hundred years from now
And I was dead and someone else was listening to them.
But I was glad I had recorded for him
    The melancholy.

Patrick Kavanagh

Four Ducks on a Pond

Four ducks on a pond,
A grass-bank beyond,
A blue sky of Spring,
White clouds on the wing;
What a little thing
To remember for years –
To remember with tears.

William Allingham

I Meant to Do My Work Today

I meant to do my work today –
But a brown bird sang in the apple tree,
And a butterfly flitted across the field,
And all the leaves were calling me.

And the wind went sighing over the land
Tossing the grasses to and fro,
And a rainbow held out its shining hand –
So what could I do but laugh and go?

Richard LeGallienne

Tall Nettles

Tall nettles cover up, as they have done
These many springs, the rusty harrow, the plough
Long worn out, and the roller made of stone:
Only the elm butt tops the nettles now.

This corner of the farmyard I like most:
As well as any bloom upon a flower
I like the dust on the nettles, never lost
Except to prove the sweetness of a shower.

Edward Thomas

'My son aged three'

My son aged three fell in the nettle bed.
'Bed' seemed a curious name for those green spears,
That regiment of spite behind the shed:
It was no place for rest. With sobs and tears
The boy came seeking comfort and I saw
White blisters beaded on his tender skin.
We soothed him till his pain was not so raw.
At last he offered us a watery grin,
And then I took my billhook, honed the blade
And went outside and slashed in fury with it
Till not a nettle in that fierce parade
Stood upright anymore. And then I lit
A funeral pyre to burn the fallen dead,
But in two weeks the busy sun and rain
Had called up tall recruits behind the shed:
My son would often feel sharp wounds again.

Vernon Scannell

The Birderman

Most weekends, starting in the spring
Until late summer, I spend angling.
Not for fish. I find that far too tame
But for birds, a much more interesting game.

A juicy worm I use as bait
Cast a line into the tree and wait.
Seldom for long (that's half the fun)
A commotion in the leaves, the job's half done.

Pull hard, jerk home the hook
Then reel him in. Let's have a look ...
A tiny thing, a fledgling, young enough to spare.
I show mercy. Unhook, and toss it to the air.

It flies nestwards and disappears among the leaves
(What man roasts and braises, he too reprieves).
What next? A magpie. Note the splendid tail.
I wring its neck. Though stringy, it'll pass for quail.

Unlike water, the depths of trees are high
So, standing back, I cast into the sky
And ledger there beyond the topmost bough,
Until threshing down, like a black cape, screams a crow.

Evil creature! A witch in feathered form.
I try to net the dark, encircling storm.
It caws for help. Its cronies gather round
They curse and swoop. I hold my ground.

An infernal mass, a black, horrific army
I'll not succumb to Satan's origami.
I reach into my coat, I've come prepared,
Bring out my pocket scarecrow – Watch out bird!

It's cross-shaped, the sign the godless fear
In a thunderflap of wings they disappear.
Except of course, that one, ungainly kite
Broken now, and quickly losing height.

I haul it in, and with a single blow
Dispatch it to that Aviary below.
The ebb and flow: magpie, thrush, nightingale and crow.
The wood darkens. Time to go.

I pack away the food I've caught
And thankful for a good day's sport
Amble home. The forest fisherman.
And I'll return as soon as I can

To bird. For I'm a birderer. The birderman.

Roger McGough

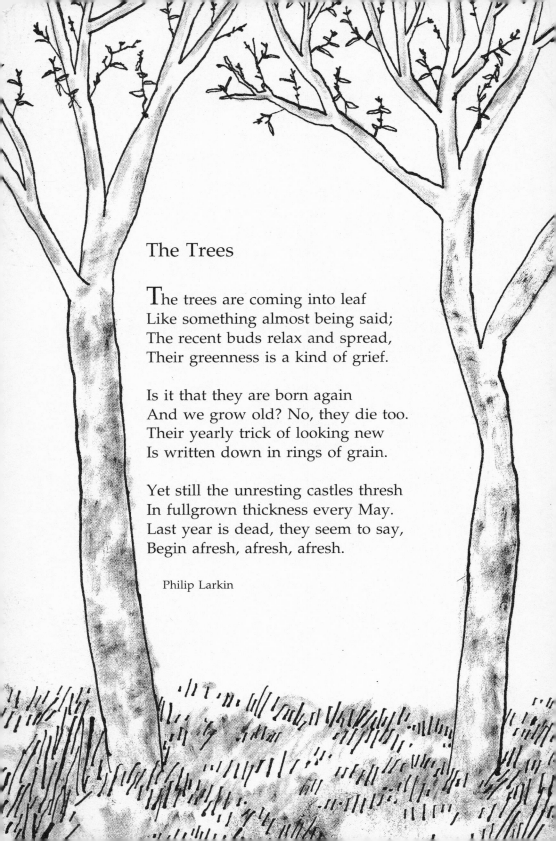

The Trees

The trees are coming into leaf
Like something almost being said;
The recent buds relax and spread,
Their greenness is a kind of grief.

Is it that they are born again
And we grow old? No, they die too.
Their yearly trick of looking new
Is written down in rings of grain.

Yet still the unresting castles thresh
In fullgrown thickness every May.
Last year is dead, they seem to say,
Begin afresh, afresh, afresh.

Philip Larkin

Millions of Strawberries

Marcia and I went over the curve,
Eating our way down
Jewels of strawberries we didn't deserve,
Eating our way down,
Till our hands were sticky, and our lips painted.
And over us the hot day fainted,
And we saw snakes,
And got scratched,
And a lust overcame us for the red unmatched
Small buds of berries,
Till we lay down –
Eating our way down –
And rolled in the berries like two little dogs,
Rolled
In the late gold.
And gnats hummed,
And it was cold,
And home we went, home without a berry,
Painted red and brown,
Eating our way down.

Genevieve Taggard

The Garden Fairy
(a true story)

I saw a little girl
She was watching her father
He was taking rocks from the garden
And dumping them in the river
Her mother called
'What is Daddy doing?'
'He's trying to make the garden lighter.'

Spike Milligan

The Pasture

I'm going out to clean the pasture spring;
I'll only stop to rake the leaves away
(And wait to watch the water clear, I may):
I shan't be gone long. – You come too.

I'm going out to fetch the little calf
That's standing by the mother. It's so young
It totters when she licks it with her tongue.
I shan't be gone long. – You come too.

Robert Frost

Pleasant Sounds

The rustling of leaves under the feet in woods and under
   hedges;
The crumping of cat-ice and snow down wood-rides,
   narrow lanes, and every street causeway;
Rustling through a wood or rather rushing, while the wind
   halloos in the oak-top like thunder;
The rustle of birds' wings startled from their nests or flying
   unseen into the bushes;
The whizzing of larger birds overhead in a wood, such as
   crows, puddocks, buzzards;
The trample of robins and woodlarks on the brown leaves,
   and the patter of squirrels on the green moss;
The fall of an acorn on the ground, the pattering of nuts on
   the hazel branches as they fall from ripeness;
The flirt of the groundlark's wing from the stubbles – how
   sweet such pictures on dewy mornings, when the dew
   flashes from its brown feathers!

John Clare

A Hot Day

Cotton-wool clouds loiter.
A lawn mower very far
Birrs. Then a bee comes
To a crimson rose and softly,
Deftly and fatly crams
A velvet body in.

A. S. J. Tessimond

The Sick Rose

O Rose, thou art sick.
The invisible worm,
That flies in the night
In the howling storm:

Has found out thy bed
Of crimson joy:
And his dark secret love
Does thy life destroy.

William Blake

The Way through the Woods

They shut the road through the woods
Seventy years ago.
Weather and rain have undone it again,
And now you would never know
There was once a road through the woods
Before they planted the trees.
It is underneath the coppice and heath,
And the thin anemones.
Only the keeper sees
That, where the ring-dove broods,
And the badgers roll at ease,
There was once a road through the woods.

Yet, if you enter the woods
Of a summer evening late,
When the night-air cools on the trout-ringed pools
Where the otter whistles his mate,
(They fear not men in the woods,
Because they see so few.)
You will hear the beat of a horse's feet,
And the swish of a skirt in the dew,
Steadily cantering through
The misty solitudes,
As though they perfectly knew
The old lost road through the woods ...
But there is no road through the woods!

Rudyard Kipling

Autumn

Autumn arrives
Like an experienced robber
Grabbing the green stuff
Then cunningly covering his tracks
With a deep multitude
Of colourful distractions.
And the wind,
The wind is his accomplice
Putting an air of chaos
Into the careful diversions
So branches shake
And dead leaves are suddenly blown
In the faces of inquisitive strangers.
The theft chills the world
Changes the temper of the earth
Till the normally placid sky
Glows red with a quiet rage.

Alan Bold

Late Autumn Poem

birdless, and
almost bared,
  Trees,
  twigs chattering,
    squeeze the last drops
      out of the sun
        and rub them
          deep into parts
            only trees know about.

Roger McGough

The Trees Dance

Forest-father, mighty Oak:
On my back the lightning-stroke

Spear-maker, Ash-tree:
Safely cross the raging sea

Black-eyed Elder, crooked-arm:
Break me and you'll come to harm

Dark Yew, poison-cup:
Keep the ghosts from rising up

Summer's herald, Hawthorn, May:
Home of the fairies, keep away

Cry-a-leaf, the bitter Willow:
Where you walk at night I follow

Slender Hazel, water-hound:
In my nutshell wisdom found

Birch the dancer, best broom:
Sweep the evil from your room

Fair Apple, fire's sweet wood:
Dreams of power and poets' food

Winter-shiner, Holly the king:
Good cheer to the cold I bring

Rowan the guard, berry-red:
Fairies fear and witches dread

Libby Houston

The Wind

The wind is a dog
flattening all this tall grass
before lying down.

Kevin Hart

Allie

Allie, call the birds in,
   The birds from the sky!
Allie calls, Allie sings,
   Down they all fly:
First there came
Two white doves,
   Then a sparrow from his nest,
Then a clucking bantam hen,
   Then a robin red-breast.

Allie, call the beasts in,
   The beasts, every one!
Allie calls, Allie sings,
   In they all run:
First there came
Two black lambs,
   Then a grunting Berkshire sow,
then a dog without a tail,
   Then a red and white cow.

Allie, call the fish up,
   The fish from the stream!
Allie calls, Allie sings,
   Up they all swim:
First there came
Two goldfish,
   A minnow and a miller's thumb,
Then a school of little trout,
   Then the twisting eels come.

Allie, call the children,
　　Call them from the green!
Allie calls, Allie sings,
　　Soon they run in:
First there came
Tom and Madge,
　　Kate and I who'll not forget
How we played by the water's edge
　　Till the April sun set.

Robert Graves

Conceit

I heard a winter tree in song
Its leaves were birds, a hundred strong;
When all at once it ceased to sing,
For every leaf had taken wing.

Mervyn Peake

Thaw

Over the land freckled with snow half-thawed
The speculating rooks at their nests cawed
And saw from elm-tops, delicate as flower of grass,
What we below could not see, Winter pass.

Edward Thomas

Windy Nights

Whenever the moon and the stars are set,
 Whenever the wind is high,
All night long in the dark and wet
 A man goes riding by.
Late in the night when the fires are out,
Why does he gallop and gallop about?

Whenever the trees are crying aloud,
 And ships are tossed at sea,
By, in the highway, low and loud,
 By at the gallop goes he.
By at the gallop he goes, and then
By at the gallop he comes back again.

Robert Louis Stevenson

Kite

I'm
part of a
project on flight.
I'm supposed to attain
a great height. But
unfortunately
I got stuck
in a tree
so
it
looks
like
I'm
here
for
the
night!

June Crebbin

No!

No sun – no moon!
No morn – no noon –
No dawn – no dusk – no proper time of day –
No sky – no earthly view –
No distance looking blue –
No road – no street – no 't'other side the way' –
No end to any Row –
No indications where the Crescents go –
No top to any steeple –
No recognitions of familiar people –
No courtesies for showing 'em –
No knowing 'em! –
No travelling at all – no locomotion,
No inkling of the way – no notion –
'No go' – by land or ocean –
No mail – no post –
No news from any foreign coast –
No Park – no Ring – no afternoon gentility –
No company – no nobility –
No warmth, no cheerfulness, no healthful ease,
No comfortable feel in any member –
No shade, no shine, no butterflies, no bees,
No fruits, no flowers, no leaves, no birds, –
November!

Thomas Hood

The Fog

I saw the fog grow thick
   Which soon made blind my ken;
It made tall men of boys,
   And giants of tall men.

It clutched my throat, I coughed;
   Nothing was in my head
Except two heavy eyes
   Like balls of burning lead.

And when it grew so black
   That I could know no place,
I lost all judgement then
   Of distance and of space.

The street lamps, and the lights
   Upon the halted cars,
Could either be on earth
   Or by the heavenly stars.

A man passed by me close,
   I asked my way, he said,
'Come, follow me, my friend' –
   I followed where he led.

He walked the stones in front,
   'Trust me,' he said, 'and come':
I followed like a child –
   A blind man led me home.

   W. H. Davies

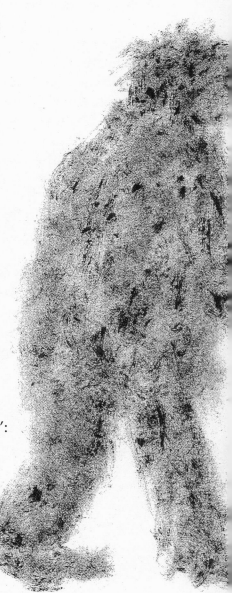

Winter

Winter crept
through the whispering wood,
hushing fir and oak;
crushed each leaf and froze each web –
but never a word he spoke.

Winter prowled
by the shivering sea,
lifting sand and stone;
nipped each limpet silently –
and then moved on.

Winter raced
down the frozen stream,
catching at his breath;
on his lips were icicles,
at his back was death.

Judith Nicholls

Red Boots On

Way down Geneva,
All along Vine,
Deeper than the snow drift
Love's eyes shine:

Mary Lou's walking
In the winter time.

She's got

Red boots on, she's got
Red boots on,
Kicking up the winter
Till the winter's gone.

So

Go by Ontario,
Look down Main,
If you can't find Mary Lou,
Come back again:

Sweet light burning
In winter's flame.

She's got

Snow in her eyes, got
A tingle in her toes
And new red boots on
Wherever she goes

So

All around Lake Street,
Up by St Paul,
Quicker than the white wind
Love takes all:

Mary Lou's walking
In the big snow fall.

She's got

Red boots on, she's got
Red boots on,
Kicking up the winter
Till the winter's gone.

Kit Wright

Stopping by Woods on a Snowy Evening

Whose woods these are I think I know.
His house is in the village though;
He will not see me stopping here
To watch his woods fill up with snow.

My little horse must think it queer
To stop without a farmhouse near
Between the woods and frozen lake
The darkest evening of the year.

He gives his harness bells a shake
To ask if there is some mistake.
The only other sound's the sweep
Of easy wind and downy flake.

The woods are lovely, dark and deep,
But I have promises to keep,
And miles to go before I sleep,
And miles to go before I sleep.

Robert Frost

Boy at the Window

Seeing the snowman standing all alone
In dusk and cold is more than he can bear.
The small boy weeps to hear the wind prepare
A night of gnashings and enormous moan.
His tearful sight can hardly reach to where
The pale-faced figure with bitumen eyes
Returns him such a god-forsaken stare
As outcast Adam gave to Paradise.

The man of snow is, nonetheless, content,
Having no wish to go inside and die.
Still, he is moved to see the youngster cry.
Though frozen water is his element,
He melts enough to drop from one soft eye
A trickle of the purest rain, a tear
For the child at the bright pane surrounded by
Such warmth, such light, such love, and so much fear.

Richard Wilbur

Snowball

More snow fell that week
than had fallen for thirty years.
The cold squeezed like a bully's hug
and made you grin at nothing.

Andrew Pond and Davy Rickers and me
went out,
three sprats, into the white bite of the world.
We shared my balaclava.

And for an hour we chucked snowballs
at the windows on our estate;
spattered the pristine panes of Nelson Way,
powdered the gleaming glass up Churchill Drive,
until we got bored
and Andrew Pond's mitts from his Granny
shrank.

It was me who started it off,
that last snowball,
rolling it from the size of a 50p scoop,
down Thatcher Hill,
to the size of a spacehopper.
It creaked under my gloves as I pushed.
Then Dave Rickers and Andrew Pond joined in,
and we shoved the thing
the length of Wellington Road.
It groaned as it grew
and grew.

The size of a sleeping polar bear.
The size of an igloo.
The size,
by the time we turned the corner
into the road where I lived,
of a full moon –
the three of us astronauts.

The worst of it was
that Andrew Pond and Davy Rickers ran off,
leaving me
dwarfed and alarmed
by a planet of snow
on our front lawn.
It went so dark in our living-room,
I was later to hear,
that my mother thought there had been an eclipse.

And later that night –
after the terrible telling-off,
red-eyed,
supperless –
I stared from my bedroom window
at the enormity of my crime,
huge and luminous
under the ice-cold stars.
To tell the truth,
It was pride that I felt,
even though
I had to stop in for as long as it took
for the snowball to melt.

Carol Ann Duffy

The Small Window

In Wales there are jewels
To gather, but with the eye
Only. A hill lights up
Suddenly; a field trembles
With colour and goes out
In its turn; in one day
You can witness the extent
Of the spectrum and grow rich

With looking. Have a care;
This wealth is for the few
And chosen. Those who crowd
A small window dirty it
With their breathing, though sublime
And inexhaustible the view.

R. S. Thomas

My Heart's in the Highlands

My heart's in the Highlands, my heart is not here;
My heart's in the Highlands a-chasing the deer;
Chasing the wild deer, and following the roe,
My heart's in the Highlands wherever I go.
Farewell to the Highlands, farewell to the North,
The birth-place of valour, the country of worth;
Wherever I wander, wherever I rove,
The hills of the Highlands for ever I love.

Farewell to the mountains, high covered with snow;
Farewell to the straths and green valleys below;
Farewell to the forests and wild-hanging woods;
Farewell to the torrents and loud-pouring floods.
My heart's in the Highlands, my heart is not here;
My heart's in the Highlands a-chasing the deer;
Chasing the wild deer, and following the roe,
My heart's in the Highlands, wherever I go.

Robert Burns

Conservation Piece

The countryside must be preserved!
(Preferably miles away from me.)
Neat hectares of the stuff reserved
For those in need of flower or tree.

I'll make do with landscape painting
Film documentaries on TV.
And when I need to escape, panting,
Then open-mouthed I'll head for the sea.

Let others stroll and take their leisure,
In grasses wade up to their knees,
For I derive no earthly pleasure
From the green green rash that makes me sneeze.

Roger McGough

Song of the City

My brain is stiff with concrete
My limbs are rods of steel
My belly's stuffed with money
My soul was bought in a deal.

They poured metal through my arteries
They choked my lungs with lead
They churned my blood to plastic
They put murder in my head.

I'd a face like a map of the weather
Flesh that grew to the bone
But they tore my story out of my eyes
And turned my heart to stone.

Let me wind from my source like a river
Let me grow like wheat from the grain
Let me hold out my arms like a natural tree
Let my children love me again.

Gareth Owen

The River's Story

I remember when life was good.
I shilly-shallied across meadows,
Tumbled down mountains,
I laughed and gurgled through woods,
Stretched and yawned in a myriad of floods.
Insects, weightless as sunbeams,
Settled upon my skin to drink.
I wore lily-pads like medals.
Fish, lazy and battle-scarred,
Gossiped beneath them.
The damselflies were my ballerinas,
The pike my ambassadors.
Kingfishers, disguised as rainbows,
Were my secret agents.
It was a sweet time, a gone-time,
A time before factories grew,
Brick by greedy brick,
And left me cowering
In monstrous shadows.
Like drunken giants
They vomited their poisons into me.
Tonight a scattering of vagrant bluebells,
Dwarfed by those same poisons,
Toll my ending.

Children, come and find me if you wish,
I am your inheritance.
Behind the derelict housing-estates
You will discover my remnants.
Clogged with garbage and junk
To an open sewer I've shrunk.

I, who have flowed through history,
Who have seen hamlets become villages,
Villages become towns, towns become cities,
Am reduced to a trickle of filth
Beneath the still, burning stars.

Brian Patten

Poisoned Talk

Who killed cock robin?
I, said the worm,
I did him great harm,
He died on the branch of a withered tree
From the acid soil that poisoned me.

Who killed the heron?
I, mouthed the fish,
With my tainted flesh
I killed tern, duck and drake,
All the birds of the lake.

Who killed the lake?
I, boasted Industry,
I poisoned with mercury
Fish, plant and weed
To pamper men's greed.

Who killed the flowers?
I, moaned the wind,
I prowl unconfined,
Blowing acid rain
Over field, flood and fen.

Who killed the forest?
I ensured that it died,
Said sulphur dioxide.
And all life within it,
From earthworm to linnet.

Raymond Wilson

The Soldiers Came

The soldiers came
and dropped their bombs.
The soldiers didn't take long
To bring the forest down.

With the forest gone
the birds are gone.
With the birds gone
who will sing their song?

But the soldiers forgot
to take the forest
out of the people's hearts.
The soldiers forgot
to take the birds
out of the people's dreams.
And in the people's dreams
the birds still sing their song.

Now the children
are planting seedlings
to help the forest grow again.
They eat a simple meal of soft rice
wrapped in banana leaf.
And the land welcomes their smiling
like a shower of rain.

John Agard

Ballad

O what is that sound which so thrills the ear
  Down in the valley drumming, drumming?
Only the scarlet soldiers, dear,
    The soldiers coming.

O what is that light I see flashing so clear
  Over the distance brightly, brightly?
Only the sun on their weapons, dear,
    As they step lightly.

O what are they doing with all that gear;
  What are they doing this morning, this morning?
Only the usual manoeuvres, dear,
    Or perhaps a warning.

O why have they left the road down there;
  Why are they suddenly wheeling, wheeling?
Perhaps a change in the orders, dear;
    Why are you kneeling?

O haven't they stopped for the doctor's care;
  Haven't they reined their horses, their horses?
Why, they are none of them wounded, dear,
    None of these forces.

O is it the parson they want with white hair;
  Is it the parson, is it, is it?
No, they are passing his gateway, dear,
    Without a visit.

O it must be the farmer who lives so near;
   It must be the farmer so cunning, so cunning?
They have passed the farm already, dear,
     And now they are running.

O where are you going? stay with me here!
   Were the vows you swore me deceiving, deceiving?
No, I promised to love you, dear,
     But I must be leaving.

O it's broken the lock and splintered the door,
   O it's the gate where they're turning, turning;
Their feet are heavy on the floor
     And their eyes are burning.

   W. H. Auden

Everything Changes
(after Brecht, *'Alles wandelt sich'*)

Everything changes. We plant
trees for those born later
but what's happened has happened,
and poisons poured into the seas
cannot be drained out again.

What's happened has happened.
Poisons poured into the seas
cannot be drained out again, but
everything changes. We plant
trees for those born later.

Cicely Herbert

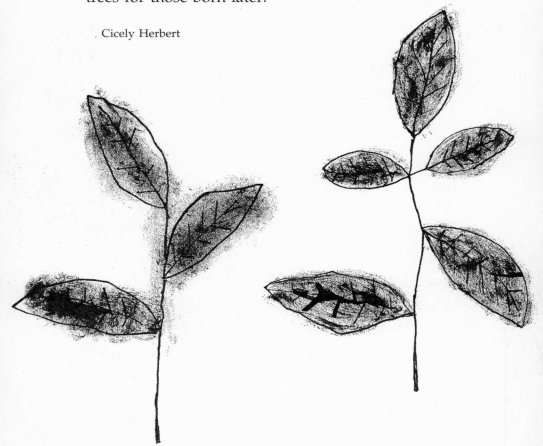

Sometimes

Sometimes things don't go, after all,
from bad to worse. Some years, muscadel
faces down frost; green thrives: the crops don't fail,
sometimes a man aims high, and all goes well.

A people sometimes will step back from war;
elect an honest man; decide they care
enough, that they can't leave some stranger poor.
Some men become what they were born for.

Sometimes our best efforts do not go
amiss; sometimes we do as we meant to.
The sun will sometimes melt a field of sorrow
that seemed hard frozen: may it happen for you.

Sheenagh Pugh

Questions at Night

Why
Is the sky?

What starts the thunder overhead?
Who makes the crashing noise?
Are the angels falling out of bed?
Are they breaking all their toys?

Why does the sun go down so soon?
Why do the night-clouds crawl
Hungrily up to the new-laid moon
And swallow it, shell and all?

If there's a Bear among the stars,
As all the people say,
Won't he jump over those pasture-bars
And drink up the Milky Way?

Does every star that happens to fall
Turn into a firefly?
Can't it ever get back to Heaven at all?
And why
Is the sky?

Louis Untermeyer

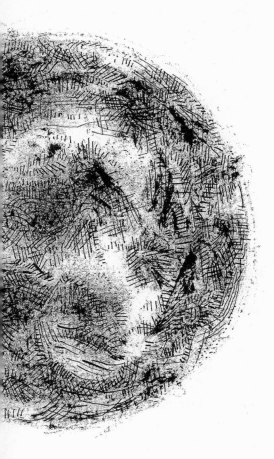

Song in Space

When man first flew beyond the sky
He looked back into the world's blue eye.
Man said: What makes your eye so blue?
Earth said: The tears in the oceans do.
Why are the seas so full of tears?
Because I've wept so many thousand years.
Why do you weep as you dance through space?
Because I am the mother of the human race.

Adrian Mitchell

Escape at Bedtime

The lights from the parlour and kitchen shone out
   Through the blinds and the windows and bars;
And high overhead and all moving about,
   There were thousands of millions of stars.
There ne'er were such thousands of leaves on a tree,
   Nor of people in church or the park,
As the crowds of the stars that looked down upon me,
   And that glittered and winked in the dark.

The Dog, and the Plough, and the Hunter, and all,
   And the star of the sailor, and Mars,
These shone in the sky, and the pail by the wall
   Would be half full of water and stars.
They saw me at last, and they chased me with cries,
   And they soon had me packed into bed;
But the glory kept shining and bright in my eyes,
   And the stars going round in my head.

Robert Louis Stevenson

Night and Stars

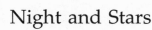
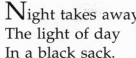

Night takes away
The light of day
In a black sack.

Bright white stars escape
Through holes they make
In the black sack
The night has on its back.

Stanley Cook

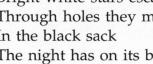

The Night Will Never Stay

The night will never stay,
The night will still go by,
Though with a million stars
You pin it to the sky;

Though you bind it with the blowing wind
And buckle it with the moon,
The night will slip away
Like sorrow or a tune.

Eleanor Farjeon

Stars and Planets

Trees are cages for them: water holds its breath
To balance them without smudging on its delicate meniscus.
Children watch them playing in their heavenly playground;
Men use them to lug ships across oceans, through firths.

They seem so twinkle-still, but they never cease
Inventing new spaces and huge explosions
And migrating in mathematical tribes over
The steppes of space at their outrageous ease.

It's hard to think that the earth is one –
This poor sad bearer of wars and disasters
Rolls-Roycing round the sun with its load of gangsters,
Attended only by the loveless moon.

Norman MacCaig

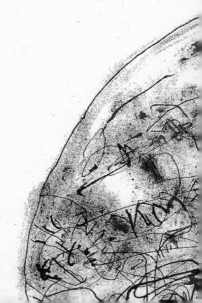

I'll Sail Upon the Dog-Star

I'll sail upon the Dog-star,
And then pursue the morning;
I'll chase the Moon till it be noon,
But I'll make her leave her horning.

I'll climb the frosty mountain,
And there I'll coin the weather;
I'll tear the rainbow from the sky
And tie both ends together.

The stars pluck from their orbs too,
And crowd them in my budget;
And whether I'm a roaring boy,
Let all the nation judge it.

Thomas Durfey

Wynken, Blynken, and Nod

Wynken, Blynken, and Nod one night
    Sailed off in a wooden shoe –
Sailed on a river of crystal light,
    Into a sea of dew.
'Where are you going, and what do you wish?'
    The old moon asked the three.
    'We have come to fish for the herring fish
    That live in this beautiful sea;
    Nets of silver and gold have we!'
        Said Wynken,
        Blynken,
        And Nod.

The old moon laughed and sang a song,
    As they rocked in the wooden shoe,
And the wind that sped them all night long
    Ruffled the waves of dew.
The little stars were the herring fish
    That lived in that beautiful sea –
    'Now cast your nets wherever you wish –
    Never afeard are we';
    So cried the stars to the fishermen three:
        Wynken,
        Blynken,
        And Nod.

All night long their nets they threw
    To the stars in the twinkling foam –
Then down from the skies came the wooden shoe,
    Bringing the fishermen home;
'Twas all so pretty a sail it seemed
    As if it could not be,
And some folks thought 'twas a dream they'd dreamed

Of sailing that beautiful sea –
But I shall name you the fishermen three:
   Wynken,
   Blynken,
   And Nod.

Wynken and Blynken are two little eyes,
   And Nod is a little head,
And the wooden shoe that sailed the skies
   Is the wee one's trundle-bed.
So shut your eyes while mother sings
   Of wonderful sights that be,
And you shall see the beautiful things
   As you rock in the misty sea,
   Where the old shoe rocked the fishermen three:
      Wynken,
      Blynken,
      And Nod.

Eugene Field

from The Bed Book

Beds come in all sizes –
Single or double,
Cot-size or cradle,
King-size or trundle.

Most Beds are Beds
For sleeping or resting,
But the *best* Beds are much
More interesting!

Not just a white little
Tucked-in-tight little
Nighty-night little
Turn-out-the-light little
    Bed –

    Instead
A Bed for Fishing,
A Bed for Cats,
A Bed for a Troupe of
    Acrobats.

The *right* sort of Bed
(If you see what I mean)
Is a Bed that might
Be a Submarine

Nosing through water
Clear and green,
Silver and glittery
As a sardine

Or a Jet-Propelled Bed
For visiting Mars
With mosquito nets
For the shooting stars ...

Sylvia Plath

Magic Story for Falling Asleep

When the last giant came out of his cave
and his bones turned into the mountain
and his clothes turned into the flowers,

nothing was left but his tooth
which my dad took home in his truck
which my granddad carved into a bed

which my mom tucks me into at night
when I dream of the last giant
when I fall asleep on the mountain

Nancy Willard

Lullaby

Hush, little baby, don't say a word,
Papa's going to buy you a mocking bird.

If the mocking bird won't sing,
Papa's going to buy you a diamond ring.

If the diamond ring turns to brass,
Papa's going to buy you a looking-glass.

If the looking-glass gets broke,
Papa's going to buy you a billy-goat.

If that billy-goat runs away,
Papa's going to buy you another today.

Anonymous

Dream Poem

I dream a dream about a door
Into the dream I dreamed before.
I turn the key, I push, and then
I see the garden once again.
The waking world around me seems
Much less real than my dreams.

I dream a dream about a child
Who plays within the garden wild,
Where bracken grows as tall as trees
And creaks in every summer breeze,
Where grasses sighing brush your face.
There are no people in the place.

But there beneath gigantic roses,
Worms as fat as garden hoses,
Beetles anoraked in steel,
Snails the size of tractor wheels,
Slugs like hoover bags gone wrong,
Millipedes a metre long.

Bees in burglars' jerseys whirr
Like chain-saws through that atmosphere.
Butterflies have alien faces
And wings the size of pillow-cases.
Pumpkin-plump, a spider waits
Beside her silver fishing nets.

I dream a pond where fishes rise
Making mouths at Paradise.
I dream a tower by the pond
And, from the top, the views beyond
The wall spread out like coloured maps
To ... where? I do not know. Perhaps

I'll climb the tower. Perhaps. I may
Tomorrow. I may not. Today
I know I do not care to care.
I watch the spider in her lair.
I watch her watch the butterfly
Who finds too soon the way to die.

John Whitworth

Round the Park

Where are you going?
  Round the park
When are you back?
  After dark

Won't you be scared?
  What a laugh
A ghost'll get you
  Don't be daft

I know where it lives
  No you don't
And you'll run away
  No I won't

It got me once
  It didn't ... did it?
It's all SLIMY
  Tisn't ... is it?

Where are you going?
  I'm staying at home
Aren't you going to the park?
  Not on my own.

Michael Rosen

To See a Ghost

To see a ghost
is to wait in a train
as another pulls in
the opposite way

and through the glass
only inches from yours
a face you almost
know from years

and years ago
stares back. Those eyes
meet yours. You blink
at each other's surprise

and see the *Oh!*
on each other's lips
as one train shudders
and begins to slip

away so smoothly
that neither can tell
which is moving,
which is still,

and who's going up,
who down, the line
and who's running on,
who out of, time.

Philip Gross

Disillusionment of Ten O'Clock

The houses are haunted
By white night-gowns.
None are green,
Or purple with green rings,
Or green with yellow rings,
Or yellow with blue rings.
None of them are strange,
With socks of lace
And beaded ceintures.
People are not going
To dream of baboons and periwinkles.
Only, here and there, an old sailor,
Drunk and asleep in his boots,
Catches tigers
In red weather.

Wallace Stevens

The Deserted House

There's no smoke in the chimney,
  And the rain beats on the floor;
There's no glass in the window,
  There's no wood in the door;
The heather grows behind the house,
  And the sand lies before.

No hand hath trained the ivy,
  The walls are grey and bare;
The boats upon the sea sail by,
  Nor ever tarry there.
No beast of the field comes nigh,
  Nor any bird of the air.

Mary Coleridge

The Listeners

'Is there anybody there?' said the Traveller,
    Knocking on the moonlit door;
And his horse in the silence champed the grasses
    Of the forest's ferny floor:
And a bird flew up out of the turret,
    Above the Traveller's head:
And he smote upon the door again a second time;
    'Is there anybody there?' he said.
But no one descended to the Traveller;
    No head from the leaf-fringed sill
Leaned over and looked into his grey eyes,
    Where he stood perplexed and still.
But only a host of phantom listeners
    That dwelt in the lone house then
Stood listening in the quiet of the moonlight
    To that voice from the world of men:
Stood thronging the faint moonbeams on the dark stair,
    That goes down to the empty hall,
Hearkening in an air stirred and shaken
    By the lonely Traveller's call.
And he felt in his heart their strangeness,
    Their stillness answering his cry,
While his horse moved, cropping the dark turf,
    'Neath the starred and leafy sky;
For he suddenly smote on the door, even
    Louder, and lifted his head:
'Tell them I came, and no one answered,
    That I kept my word,' he said.
Never the least stir made the listeners,
    Though every word he spake
Fell echoing through the shadowiness of the still house
    From the one man left awake:

Ay, they heard his foot upon the stirrup,
   And the sound of iron on stone,
And how the silence surged softly backward,
   When the plunging hoofs were gone.

   Walter de la Mare

Green Man in the Garden

Green man in the garden
   Staring from the tree,
Why do you look so long and hard
   Through the pane at me?

Your eyes are dark as holly,
   Of sycamore your horns,
Your bones are made of elder-branch,
   Your teeth are made of thorns.

Your hat is made of ivy-leaf,
   Of bark your dancing shoes,
And evergreen and green and green
   Your jacket and shirt and trews.

Leave your house and leave your land
   And throw away the key,
And never look behind, he creaked,
   And come and live with me.

I bolted up the window,
   I bolted up the door,
I drew the blind that I should find
   The green man never more.

But when I softly turned the stair
   As I went up to bed,
I saw the green man standing there.
   Sleep well, my friend, he said.

Charles Causley

All of Us

All of us are afraid
More often than we tell.

There are times we cling like mussels to the sea-wall,
And pray that the pounding waves
Won't smash our shell.

Times we hear nothing but the sound
Of our loneliness, like a cracked bell
From fields far away where the trees are in icy shade.

O many a time in the night-time and in the day,
More often than we say,
We are afraid.

If people say they are never frightened,
I don't believe them.
If people say they are frightened,
I want to retrieve them
From that dark shivering haunt
Where they don't want to be,
Nor I.

Let's make of ourselves, therefore, an enormous sky
Over whatever
We most hold dear.

And we'll comfort each other,
Comfort each other's
Fear.

   Kit Wright

Ozymandias

I met a traveller from an antique land
Who said: Two vast and trunkless legs of stone
Stand in the desert ... Near them, on the sand,
Half sunk, a shattered visage lies, whose frown,
And wrinkled lip, and sneer of cold command,
Tell that its sculptor well those passions read
Which yet survive, stamped on these lifeless things,
The hand that mocked them, and the heart that fed:
And on the pedestal these words appear:
'My name is Ozymandias, king of kings:
Look on my works, ye Mighty, and despair!'
Nothing beside remains. Round the decay
Of that colossal wreck, boundless and bare
The lone and level sands stretch far away.

Percy Bysshe Shelley

One Art

The art of losing isn't hard to master;
so many things seem filled with the intent
to be lost that their loss is no disaster.

Lose something every day. Accept the fluster
of lost door keys, the hour badly spent.
The art of losing isn't hard to master.

Then practice losing farther, losing faster:
places, and names, and where it was you meant
to travel. None of these will bring disaster.

I lost my mother's watch. And look! my last, or
next-to-last, of three loved houses went.
The art of losing isn't hard to master.

I lost two cities, lovely ones. And, vaster,
some realms I owned, two rivers, a continent.
I miss them, but it wasn't a disaster.

– Even losing you (the joking voice, a gesture
I love) I shan't have lied. It's evident
the art of losing's not too hard to master
though it may look like (*Write* it!) like disaster.

Elizabeth Bishop

On His Thirty-Third Birthday

More than thirty years have rushed
By me like a runaway
Chariot. I too have spent
My life rushing here and there
From one end of the country
To the other. I long for
The homestead where I was born,
A thousand mountain ranges
Away. Like yellow leaves in
The decline of Summer a
Few white hairs have already
Appeared on my head. All my
Travels only made tracks
In drifting sand. I piled up
Learning like a snowball.
I crossed mountains and passed
Examinations and gave
Learned speeches. What did I gain?
Better I stayed home
And raised prize melons.

Ch'ang Kuo Fan

(*translated from the Chinese by Kenneth Rexroth*)

'Weary, I tear open the shopping'

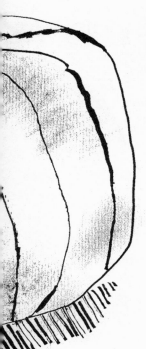

Weary, I tear open the shopping.
From the newspaper waddles
on the table
                like an irate duck
this melon.

Robert Gray

Transformation

I saw an old woman, squat and wrinkled and sallow,
her swift step shrunk to a snail's pace,
and who would believe her hair had once been yellow?

But her husband spoke to her softly, and took her arm,
and I saw the girl's eyes in the aged face,

And I saw that time can be a cruel enchanter,
but love is the true charm
to break all spells that a princess may encounter.

Evangeline Paterson

You Are Old, Father William

'You are old, Father William,' the young man said,
    'And your hair has become very white;
And yet you incessantly stand on your head –
    Do you think, at your age, it is right?'

'In my youth,' Father William replied to his son,
    'I feared it might injure the brain;
But now that I'm perfectly sure I have none,
    Why, I do it again and again.'

'You are old,' said the youth, 'as I mentioned before,
    And have grown most uncommonly fat;
Yet you turned a back-somersault in at the door –
    Pray, what is the reason of that?'

'In my youth,' said the sage, as he shook his grey locks,
    'I kept all my limbs very supple
By the use of this ointment – one shilling the box –
    Allow me to sell you a couple.'

'You are old,' said the youth, 'and your jaws are too weak
    For anything tougher than suet;
Yet you finished the goose, with the bones and the beak –
    Pray, how did you manage to do it?'

'In my youth,' said his father, 'I took to the law,
    And argued each case with my wife;
And the muscular strength which it gave to my jaw
    Has lasted the rest of my life.'

'You are old,' said the youth; 'one would hardly suppose
　　That your eye was as steady as ever;
Yet you balanced an eel on the end of your nose –
　　What made you so awfully clever?'

'I have answered three questions, and that is enough,'
　　Said his father; 'don't give yourself airs!
Do you think I can listen all day to such stuff?
　　Be off, or I'll kick you down stairs!'

Lewis Carroll

Fairy Tale

He built himself a house,
      his foundations,
      his stones,
      his walls,
      his roof overhead,
      his chimney and smoke,
      his view from the window.

He made himself a garden,
      his fence,
      his thyme,
      his earthworm,
      his evening dew.

He cut out his bit of sky above.

And he wrapped the garden in the sky
and the house in the garden
and packed the lot in a handkerchief

and went off
lone as an arctic fox
through the cold
unending
rain
into the world.

   Miroslav Holub

The Magpies

When Tom and Elizabeth took the farm
  The bracken made their bed,
And *Quardle oodle ardle wardle doodle*
  The magpies said.

Tom's hand was strong to the plough
  Elizabeth's lips were red,
And *Quardle oodle ardle wardle doodle*
  The magpies said.

Year in year out they worked
  While the pines grew overhead,
And *Quardle oodle ardle wardle doodle*
  The magpies said.

But all the beautiful crops soon went
  To the mortgage-man instead,
And *Quardle oodle ardle wardle doodle*
  The magpies said.

Elizabeth is dead now (it's years ago)
  Old Tom went light in the head;
And *Quardle oodle ardle wardle doodle*
  The magpies said.

The farm's still there. Mortgage corporations
  Couldn't give it away.
And *Quardle oodle ardle wardle doodle*
  The magpies say.

Denis Glover

Why Brownlee Left

Why Brownlee left, and where he went,
Is a mystery even now.
For if a man should have been content
It was him; two acres of barley,
One of potatoes, four bullocks,
A milker, a slated farmhouse.
He was last seen going out to plough
On a March morning, bright and early.

By noon Brownlee was famous;
They had found all abandoned, with
The last rig unbroken, his pair of black
Horses, like man and wife,
Shifting their weight from foot to
Foot, and gazing into the future.

Paul Muldoon

I Have Always Known

I have always known
That at last I would
Take this road, but yesterday
I did not know that it would be today.

Narihira

(*Translated by Kenneth Rexroth*)

Uphill

Does the road wind uphill all the way?
   Yes, to the very end.
Will the day's journey take the whole long day?
   From morn to night, my friend.

But is there for the night a resting-place?
   A roof for when the slow, dark hours begin.
May not the darkness hide it from my face?
   You cannot miss that inn.

Shall I meet other wayfarers at night?
   Those who have gone before.
Then must I knock, or call when just in sight?
   They will not keep you waiting at that door.

Shall I find comfort, travel-sore and weak?
   Of labour you shall find the sum.
Will there be beds for me and all who seek?
   Yea, beds for all who come.

Christina Rossetti

Daydream

One day people will touch and talk perhaps easily,
And loving be natural as breathing and warm as sunlight,
And people will untie themselves, as string is unknotted,
Unfold and yawn and stretch and spread their fingers,
Unfurl, uncurl like seaweed returned to the sea,
And work will be simple and swift as a seagull flying,
And play will be casual and quiet as a seagull settling,
And the clocks will stop, and no one will wonder or care or
    notice,
And people will smile without reason, even in the winter,
    even in the rain.

A. S. J. Tessimond

Back Home Contemplation

There is more to heaven
than meet the eye
there is more to sea
than watch the sky
there is more to earth
than dream the mind

O my eye

The heavens are blue
but the sun is murderous
the sea is calm
but the waves reap havoc
the earth is firm
but trees dance shadows
and bush eyes turn

Grace Nichols

You can go now

You can go now yes go now. Go east or west, go north or south, you can go now. Or you can go up or go down now. And after these there is no place to go. If you say no to all of them then you stay here. You don't go. You are fixed and put. And from here if you choose you send up rockets, you let down buckets. Here then for you is the centre of things.

Carl Sandburg

Spell of Creation

Within the flower there lies a seed,
Within the seed there springs a tree,
Within the tree there spreads a wood.

In the wood there burns a fire,
And in the fire there melts a stone,
Within the stone a ring of iron.

Within the ring there lies an O
Within the O there looks an eye,
In the eye there swims a sea,

And in the sea reflected sky,
And in the sky there shines the sun,
Within the sun a bird of gold.

Within the bird there beats a heart,
And from the heart there flows a song,
And in the song there sings a word.

In the word there speaks a world,
A word of joy, a world of grief,
From joy and grief there springs my love.

Oh love, my love, there springs a world,
And on the world there shines a sun
And in the sun there burns a fire,

Within the fire consumes my heart
And in my heart there beats a bird,
And in the bird there wakes an eye,

Within the eye, earth, sea and sky,
Earth, sky and sea within an O
Lie like the seed within the flower.

Kathleen Raine

Benediction

Thanks to the ear
that someone may hear

Thanks to seeing
that someone may see

Thanks to feeling
that someone may feel

Thanks to touch
that one may be touched

Thanks to flowering of white moon
and spreading shawl of black night
holding villages and cities together

James Berry

Words

Bright is the ring of words
   When the right man rings them,
Fair the fall of songs
   When the singer sings them.
Still they are carolled and said –
   On wings they are carried –
After the singer is dead
   And the maker buried.

Robert Louis Stevenson

Acknowledgements

The editor and publishers gratefully acknowledge permission to reprint copyright poems in this book as follows:

JOHN AGARD: 'The Soldiers Came' from *Laughter is an Egg* (Puffin Books, 1991), to the author c/o Caroline Sheldon Literary Agency. ALLAN AHLBERG: 'Why Must We Go to School?' from *Heard it in the Playground* (Viking, 1989), copyright © Allan Ahlberg, 1989, TO PENGUIN BOOKS LTD; 'LOST' FROM *Please Mrs Butler* (Viking, 1983), copyright © Allan Ahlberg, 1983, to Penguin Books Ltd. MAYA ANGELOU: 'Woman Work' from *And Still I Rise* (Virago Press, 1986), to Little, Brown & Company (UK). W. H. AUDEN: 'O what is that sound which so thrills the ear' from *Selected Poems* (Faber and Faber, 1979), to the publisher. MICHAEL BALDWIN: 'The Small Brown Bear' from *Poetry for Pleasure* (Macmillan Australia). GEORGE BARKER: 'And What, Said the Emperor' from *Collected Poems* (Faber and Faber, 1962), to the publisher. JAMES BERRY: 'One' from *When I Dance* (Hamish Hamilton), 'Look, No Hands' and 'Playing a Dazzler' from *Playing a Dazzler* (Puffin Books) and 'Benediction' from *Chain of Days* (Oxford University Press), to the Peters Fraser and Dunlop Group Ltd on behalf of the author. ELIZABETH BISHOP: 'One Art' from *The Complete Poems 1927–1979*, copyright © 1979, 1983 by Alice Helen Methfessel, to Farrar, Straus & Giroux Inc. ALAN BOLD: 'Autumn', © Alan Bold, to Alice Bold. DAVE CALDER: 'Where?' from *My First Has Gone Bonkers* (Blackie, 1993), © Dave Calder 1992, to the author. CHARLES CAUSLEY: 'Green Man in the Garden', 'I am the Song', 'Ballad of the Bread Man' and 'My Mother Saw a Dancing Bear' from *Collected Poems 1951–1975* (Macmillan, 1975), to David Higham Associates Ltd. PAULINE CLARKE: 'My Name Is ...' from *Silver Bells and Cockle Shells*, © Pauline Clarke 1962, to Curtis Brown, London. STANLEY COOK: 'Night and Stars' from *The Squirrel In Town* (Blackie, 1988), to the Estate of Stanley Cook. WENDY COPE: 'The Uncertainty of the Poet' from *With a Poet's Eye: A Tate Gallery Anthology* (1986), © Wendy Cope 1986. NATHALIA CRANE: 'The Janitor's Boy' from *The Janitor's Boy and Other Poems* (Thomas Seltzer, 1924). JUNE CREBBIN: 'Kite' from *The Jungle Sale* (Penguin, 1990). E. E. CUMMINGS: 'maggie and milly and molly and may' from *Complete Poems 1904–1962*, edited by George J. Firmage, copyright © 1991 by the Trustees for the E. E. Cummings Trust and George James Firmage, to W. W. Norton & Company. PHILIP DACEY: 'Thumb' from *How I Escaped from the Labyrinth* (Carnegie-Mellon University Press, 1977), to the author. W. H. DAVIES: 'The Hermit', 'The Frog' and 'The Blind Boxer' from *Collected Poems* (Jonathan Cape), to the Executors of the W. H. Davies Estate and Random House UK Ltd; WALTER DE LA MARE: 'Echo' and 'The Listeners' from *The Complete Poems of Walter de la Mare* (1969), to The Literary Trustees of Walter de la Mare, and the Society of Authors as their representative. EMILY DICKINSON: 'I Stepped from Plank to Plank' from *The Complete Poems of Emily Dickinson*, edited by Thomas H. Johnson (Little, Brown & Company, 1988), to

exhilaration' from *Moortown Diary* (Faber and Faber, 1989) and 'Mice Are Funny
Little Creatures' from *What is the Truth? A Farmyard Fable for the Young* (Faber
and Faber, 1984), to the publisher. ELIZABETH JENNINGS: 'The Radio Men'
from *Collected Poems* (Macmillan), to David Higham Associates Ltd. DONALD
JUSTICE: 'Counting the Mad' from *New and Selected Poems*, copyright © 1995 by
Donald Justice, to the author and Alfred A. Knopf Inc. PATRICK KAVANAGH:
'Wet Evening in April', to the Trustees of the Estate of Patrick Kavanagh, c/o
Peter Fallon, Literary Agent, Loughcrew, Oldcastle, Co. Meath, Ireland. JACKIE
KAY: 'Two of Everything' and 'Lovesick' from *Two's Company* (Puffin, 1992), to
Penguin Books; 'Attention Seeking' from *Three Has Gone* (Blackie Children's
Books, 1994), to the Peters Fraser and Dunlop Group Ltd on behalf of the
author. BRENDAN KENNELLY: 'Eily Kilbride' from *Book of Judas* (Bloodaxe
Books, 1991). RUDYARD KIPLING: 'A Smuggler's Song' and 'The Way through
the Woods' from *Selected Poems*, edited by Peter Keating (Penguin Twentieth
Century Classics, 1993). NAOSHI KORIYAMA: 'Unfolding Bud' from *Rhythm and
Rhyme*, edited by Elaine Hamilton (Oxford University Press Australia, 1987).
PHILIP LARKIN: 'The Trees' from *High Windows* (Faber and Faber, 1979), to the
publisher. D. H. LAWRENCE: 'People' from *Complete Poems of D. H. Lawrence*,
edited by Vivian de Sola Pinto and F. Warren Roberts (Penguin Twentieth
Century Classics, 1993), copyright © Angelo Ravagli and C. M. Weekley,
Executors of the Estate of Frieda Lawrence Ravagli, 1964, 1971. BRIAN LEE:
'Cold Feet' from Late Home (Kestrel, 1976), copyright © Brian Lee, 1976, to
Penguin Books Ltd. DENNIS LEE: 'The Coat' from *The Difficulty of Living on
Other Planets* (Macmillan of Canada, 1987), copyright © 1987 Dennis Lee, to the
author c/o Westwood Creative Artists. BRIAN MCCABE: 'The Visitors' from
Hearsay (Bodley Head), to Random House UK Ltd. NORMAN MACCAIG: 'An
Ordinary Day', 'Stars and Planets' and 'Starling on a Green Lawn' from *Collected
Poems* (Chatto & Windus, 1990), to Random House UK Ltd. ROGER MCGOUGH:
'Everything Touches' from *Lucky: A Book of Poems* (Puffin, 1994), to the Peters
Fraser & Dunlop Group Limited on behalf of the author; 'Conservation Piece',
'The Birderman' and 'Poem for a dead poet' from *Melting into the Foreground*
(Penguin, 1987), to the Peters Fraser & Dunlop Group Limited on behalf of the
author; 'The Sound Collector' from *Pillow Talk* (Puffin, 1992), to the Peters Fraser
& Dunlop Group Limited on behalf of the author. IAN MCMILLAN: 'Elephant
Dreams' from *Selected Poems* (Carcanet Press, 1987), to the publisher. JOHN
MASEFIELD: 'Sea Fever' from *Ballads and Poems* (Elkin Mathews, 1910), to the
Society of Authors as the Literary Representative of the Estate of John
Masefield. SPIKE MILLIGAN: 'The Garden Fairy' from *The Mirror Running*
(Michael Joseph, 1987), to the author. ADRIAN MITCHELL: 'Song in Space' from
Balloon Lagoon and the Magic Islands of Poetry (Orchard Books, 1997), © Adrian
Mitchell; 'The Bully' from *Blue Coffee: Poems 1985–1996* (Bloodaxe Books, 1997),
© Adrian Mitchell, to the Peters Fraser and Dunlop Group Ltd on behalf of the
author. TONY MITTON: 'St Brigid and the Baker' from *Plum* (Scholastic, 1998),
© Tony Mitton 1998, to David Higham Associates Ltd. JOHN MOLE: 'The
Shoes' from *Catching the Spider* (Blackie, 1990), to the author. OSWALD

'Advice to Young Children' from *The Collected Poems of Stevie Smith* (Penguin Twentieth Century Classics), to James MacGibbon. WALLACE STEVENS: 'Disillusionment of Ten O'Clock' from *Collected Poems of Wallace Stevens* (Faber and Faber, 1984), to the publisher. MATTHEW SWEENEY: 'A Boy', 'Only the Wall' and 'The Nobody on the Hill' from *Fatso in the Red Suit* (Faber and Faber), to the publisher. GEORGE SZIRTES: 'A Small Girl Swinging' from *Selected Poems 1976–1996* (Oxford University Press) and 'Riddle' from *The Red-All-Over Riddle Book* (Faber, 1997), to the author. GENEVIEVE TAGGARD: 'Millions of Strawberries', originally published in *The New Yorker*, copyright 1929, copyright renewed, to Marsha D. Liles. A. S. J. TESSIMOND: 'Daydream' from *The Collected Poems of A. S. J. Tessimond* (Whiteknights Press, 1985); 'A Hot Day' from *Poetry for Pleasure* (Macmillan Australia). R. S. THOMAS: 'The Small Window' and 'The Sea' from *Collected Poems 1945–1990* (Dent, 1993), to the Orion Publishing Group. LOUIS UNTERMEYER: 'Questions at Night' from *The Golden Treasury of Children's Verses*, edited by Louis Untermeyer (Collins). SYLVIA TOWNSEND WARNER: 'Wish in Spring' from *Collected Poems* (Carcanet Press, 1985), to the publisher. JOHN WHITWORTH: 'Dream Poem' from *The Complete Poetical Works of Phoebe Flood* (Hodder Children's Books, 1997), to the author. RICHARD WILBUR: 'Boy at the Window' from *New and Collected Poems* (Faber and Faber, 1989), to the publisher. NANCY WILLARD: 'Magic story for falling asleep' from *Water Walker* (Alfred A. Knopf), to the author; 'The King of Cats Sends a Postcard to His Wife' from *A Visit to William Blake's Inn: Poems for Innocent and Experienced Travelers* (Harcourt Brace & Co.), to the author. RAYMOND WILSON: 'Poisoned Talk', to Mrs G. M. Wilson. CHARLES WRIGHT: 'New Poem' from *Country Music: Selected Early Poems* (Wesleyan University Press), © 1982 by Charles Wright, to University Press of New England. KIT WRIGHT: 'Cleaning Ladies' from *Hot Dog and Other Poems* (Puffin, 1982), 'All of Us' from *Great Snakes* (Puffin), 'Red Boots On' from *The Bear Looked over the Mountain* (Salamander Press) and 'Grandad' from *Rabbiting On* (Collins), to the author.

Every effort has been made to obtain permission from all copyright holders whose material is included in this book, but in some cases this has not proved possible. We wish to thank those authors who are included without acknowledgement. Faber and Faber apologize for any errors or omissions in the above list and would be grateful to be notified of any corrections that should be incorporated in the next edition of this volume.

Index of Poets